BARRON'S BOOK NOTES

GEORGE ORWELL'S

Animal Farm

BY

David Ball
Professor of French and Comparative Literature
Smith College

SERIES EDITOR

Michael Spring
Editor, *Literary Cavalcade*
Scholastic Inc.

BARRON'S EDUCATIONAL SERIES, INC.

ACKNOWLEDGMENTS

We would like to acknowledge the many painstaking hours of work Holly Hughes and Thomas F. Hirsch have devoted to making the *Book Notes* series a success.

All inquiries should be addressed to:
Barron's Educational Series, Inc.
250 Wireless Boulevard
Hauppauge, New York 11788

Library of Congress Catalog Card No. 84-18434

International Standard Book No. 0-8120-3402-3

Library of Congress Cataloging in Publication Data
Ball, David, 1942–
    George Orwell's Animal farm.

    (Barron's book notes)
    Bibliography: p. 96
    Summary: A guide to reading "Animal Farm" with a
critical and appreciative mind. Includes background
on the author's life and times, sample tests, term
paper suggestions, and a reading list.
    1. Orwell, George, 1903–1950.   Animal farm.
    [1. Orwell, George, 1903–1950.   Animal farm.
    2. English literature—History and criticism]
    I. Title.   II. Series.
PR6029.R8A725   1984   823'.912   84-18434
ISBN 0-8120-3402-3 (pbk.)

PRINTED IN THE UNITED STATES OF AMERICA

456   550   98765

CONTENTS

HOW TO USE THIS BOOK

You have to know how to approach literature in order to get the most out of it. This *Barron's Book Notes* volume follows a plan based on methods used by some of the best students to read a work of literature.

Begin with the guide's section on the author's life and times. As you read, try to form a clear picture of the author's personality, circumstances, and motives for writing the work. This background usually will make it easier for you to hear the author's tone of voice, and follow where the author is heading.

Then go over the rest of the introductory material—such sections as those on the plot, characters, setting, themes, and style of the work. Underline, or write down in your notebook, particular things to watch for, such as contrasts between characters and repeated literary devices. At this point, you may want to develop a system of symbols to use in marking your text as you read. (Of course, you should only mark up a book you own, not one that belongs to another person or a school.) Perhaps you will want to use a different letter for each character's name, a different number for each major theme of the book, a different color for each important symbol or literary device. Be prepared to mark up the pages of your book as you read. Put your marks in the margins so you can find them again easily.

Now comes the moment you've been waiting for—the time to start reading the work of literature. You may want to put aside your *Barron's Book Notes* volume until you've read the work all the way through. Or you may want to alternate, reading the *Book Notes* analysis of each section as soon as you have finished reading the corresponding part of the original. Before you move on, reread crucial passages you don't fully understand. (Don't take this guide's analysis for granted—make up your own mind as to what the work means.)

Once you've finished the whole work of literature, you may want to review it right away, so you can firm up your ideas about what it means. You may want to leaf through the book concentrating on passages you marked in reference to one character or one theme. This is also a good time to reread the *Book Notes* introductory material, which pulls together insights on specific topics.

When it comes time to prepare for a test or to write a paper, you'll already have formed ideas about the work. You'll be able to go back through it, refreshing your memory as to the author's exact words and perspective, so that you can support your opinions with evidence drawn straight from the work. Patterns will emerge, and ideas will fall into place; your essay question or term paper will almost write itself. Give yourself a dry run with one of the sample tests in the guide. These tests present both multiple-choice and essay questions. An accompanying section gives answers to the multiple-choice questions as well as suggestions for writing the essays. If you have to select a term paper topic, you may choose one from the list of suggestions in this book. This guide also provides you with a reading list, to help you when you start research for a term paper, and a selection of provocative comments by critics, to spark your thinking before you write.

THE AUTHOR AND HIS TIMES

George Orwell was a quiet, decent Englishman who passionately hated two things: inequality and political lying. Out of his hatred of inequality came a desire for a society in which class privileges would not exist. This to him was "democratic socialism." His hatred of political lying and his support for socialism led him to denounce the political lie that what was going on in the Soviet Union had anything to do with socialism. As long as people equated the Soviet Union with socialism, he felt, no one could appreciate what democratic socialism might be like.

And so, he says, he "thought of exposing the Soviet myth in a story that could be easily understood by almost anyone and which could be easily translated into other languages." That story was *Animal Farm*, and it has been translated into many other languages. Understanding Orwell's political convictions—and how they developed—will greatly enrich your reading of *Animal Farm*.

He was born Eric Blair—he took the name George Orwell many years later—in 1903, in India. His father was an important British civil servant in that country, which was then part of the British Empire. He retired on a modest pension and moved back to England a few years after Eric was born. Thus the family was part of the "lower upper-middle-classes," as Orwell was to say: people in the English upper classes who weren't rich, but who felt they should live as the upper classes traditionally did. That's why, when Eric was eight, the Blairs sent him away to boarding school to prepare for Eton, an exclusive prep school. Eric had a scholarship, and yet his father still ended up spending almost a quarter of his pension to send his son to that boarding school! From his parents' point of view, the sacrifice paid off: Eric won a scholarship to Eton. From the boy's point of view, it meant that in a ferociously snobbish, class-conscious world, he twice had the humiliating experience of being the poorest boy in the school. "In a world where the prime necessities were money, titled relatives, athleticism, tailor-made clothes . . . I was no good," he wrote years later, in a powerful essay on his school experiences called "Such, Such Were the Joys." In his first school, he was repeatedly beaten with a cane for being "no good" in various ways. And he was made to feel ashamed for "living off the bounty" of the headmaster-owner, that is, for having a scholarship. From the age of eight to eighteen, the boy learned a lot about inequality and oppression in British schools.

He graduated from Eton at eighteen, near the bottom of his class. There was no chance of a scholarship to Oxford, so Eric followed in his father's footsteps and passed the Empire's Civil Service Examination. As a member of the Imperial Police in British-ruled Burma, he was to see inequality and oppression from another point of view—from the top. The fact that he was a part of that top intensified the feelings of distance and anger that he already had toward his own class. After five years in Burma he resigned.

When he came back to Europe in 1927, he lived for more than a year in Paris, writing novels and short stories that nobody published. When his money ran out, he had to find work as a teacher, a private tutor, and even as a dishwasher. He was poor—but of his own choice. His family could have sent him the money to get back to England and find a better job than dishwashing in a Paris hotel. Perhaps he was too proud to ask for help. But there was another, deeper reason: he felt guilty for the job he had done in Burma—for having been part of an oppressive government. He saw his years of poverty as punishment—and as a way to understand the problems of the oppressed and helpless by becoming one of them.

By 1933 he had come up from the bottom enough to write a book about it: *Down and Out in Paris and London*. Probably to save his family embarrassment, Eric asked that the book be published under a pen name. He suggested a few to his publisher. One of them was the name of a river he loved: Orwell. The next year, "George Orwell" published *Burmese Days*, a sad, angry novel about his experiences there. Two more novels followed.

In 1936 came another significant experience in Orwell's life. His publisher sent him to the English coal-mining country to write about it. Here he again saw poverty close up—not the "picturesque" poverty of Paris streets and English tramps, but the dreary poverty of tough men killing themselves in the dark mines day after day, or—worse still—hungry and out of work. He wrote a powerful piece of first-hand reporting about what he saw there: *The Road to Wigan Pier*.

Afterwards, Orwell described himself as "pro-Socialist," yet he was often bitterly critical of British socialists. To refuse to "join" his own side, to insist instead on telling the unpleasant truth as he saw it, was to become an Orwell trademark.

In 1937, however, Orwell did join a side he believed in, and it almost cost him his life: he volunteered to fight for the Republic in the Spanish Civil War.

Fascism was rising in Europe: Mussolini had taken power in Italy, Hitler in Germany. In Spain, where a shaky democratic Republic had recently been born, a socialist government was elected, promising land reform, voting reform, and separation of Church and State. A group of right-wing generals led by Francisco Franco revolted against the Republic with their armies. The government was forced to arm factory workers to defend itself against the armies—and a long, bloody civil war began.

Three experiences were crucial for Orwell in the Spanish Civil War. The first was what he saw when he got there. In Barcelona, Orwell found an exhilarating atmosphere of "comradeship and respect," everyone addressing each other as "comrade," treating each other as equals. The same thing was true, he said, of the militia group he joined. Orwell believed he was seeing the success of socialism in action.

The second thing that marked Orwell was what happened to his fellow fighters. They were jailed and shot—not by Franco, but by their own "comrades," Communist-dominated elements of the same Republican government they were fighting for! The Communists disagreed with some of the views of the militia group Orwell belonged to; they suspected the men of being disloyal to Communist ideas. Luckily for Orwell, he was not rounded up with his fellow soldiers. He had been shot through the throat on the front lines and was shipped back to England for treatment.

The third experience that would stay with Orwell for the rest of his life was what happened when he returned to England and reported what he had seen. None of the socialists wanted to hear it; nobody believed it. He was an eyewitness? No matter. It was not the right time to say something that might hurt the Republican side.

So Orwell had seen the socialist ideal in action, and he had seen it crushed—not by its natural enemies on the Right, but by Communists on the Left. And he had seen the infuriating incapacity of the Left, even the non-Communist Left, to accept that truth. All of this was very much on his mind when, in the middle of World War II, he resigned his job on the BBC (the Army wouldn't take him because of his bad lungs) and began writing *Animal Farm,* in November 1943.

Once again it looked like the wrong time for a story to "expose the Soviet myth." The Soviet Union was Britain's ally in the war against Nazi Germany. And in fact four publishers would turn down *Animal Farm.* But what was "the Soviet myth"? Why did enlightened, humane people not want to believe ill of the Soviet Union? To see what *Animal Farm* is about, we must look at what happened in Russia, and what it meant for people who were in many ways Orwell's political friends.

The Russian Revolution

Ideas play a part in any revolution, but the Bolshevik Revolution of October 1917—the one that changed "Russia" into the "U.S.S.R."—was noteworthy for being principally inspired by one idea. It was a revolution consciously made in the name of one class (the working class, the "proletariat") and against another class (the owners, the "bourgeoisie"). The Revolution was made by men who believed with Karl Marx that the whole history of the world was the history of a struggle between classes—between oppressors and oppressed.

Marx, like other socialist thinkers of the 19th century, denounced the cruel injustices of industrial capitalist society as he saw it. He had a vision of ending "the exploitation of man by man" and establishing a classless society, in which all people would be equal. The only means to this end, he thought, was a revolution of the exploited (the proletariat) against the exploiters (the bourgeoisie), so that workers would own the means of production, such as the factories and machinery. This revolution would set up a "dictatorship of the proletariat" to do away with the old bourgeois order (the capitalist system) and eventually replace it with a classless society.

Lenin took this idea and further focused on the role of the Communist Party as the leader of the working class.

When Lenin reached Russia in 1917 a first revolution against the crumbling regime of the Czar had already taken place. The new government was democratic, but "bourgeois." Lenin victoriously headed the radical socialist (Bolshevik) revolution in October of that year. This was immediately followed by four years of bloody civil war: the Revolution's Red Army, organized and led by Leon Trotsky, had to defeat the "Whites" (Russians loyal to the Czar or just hostile to the Communists) and foreign troops, too.

At Lenin's death in 1924, there was a struggle between Joseph Stalin and Trotsky for leadership of the Communist Party and thus of the nation. In 1925, Stalin clearly gained the upper hand; in 1927, he was able to expel Trotsky from the Party. Later Trotsky was exiled, then deported, and finally assassinated in Mexico, probably by a Stalinist agent, in 1940. All this time, Stalin never stopped denouncing Trotsky as a traitor.

Power in the Soviet Union became increasingly concentrated in Stalin's hands. In the 1930s, massive arrests and a series of public trials not only eliminated all possible opposition, but loyal Bolsheviks and hundreds of thousands of other absolutely innocent Russians.

Still, people all over the world who felt the pull of Marx's ideal—an end to exploitation and oppression, as they saw it—thought of the Soviet Union as the country of the Revolution. It was hard for many people on the Left (who think of themselves as on the side of the exploited, and want major changes in society to attain social justice) to give up this loyalty. That's one reason why Orwell wrote *Animal Farm*.

THE FABLE

The Plot

One night when Farmer Jones has gone to bed drunk, all the animals of Manor Farm assemble in the barn for a meeting. Old Major, the prize pig, wants to tell them about a strange dream he had. First, he tells them in clear, powerful language "the nature of life" as he has come to understand it. Animals toil, suffer, get barely enough to eat; as soon as they are no longer useful, they are slaughtered. And why? Because animals are enslaved by Man, "the only creature that consumes without producing." There is only one solution: Man must be removed. And animals must be perfectly united for their common goal: Rebellion.

After a brief interruption caused by the dogs chasing after some rats and a vote proposed by Major to decide if rats are comrades (they are), Major sums up: All animals are friends, Man is the enemy. Animals must avoid Man's habits: no houses, beds, clothes, alcohol, money, trade. Above all, "we are brothers. No animal must ever kill any other animal. All animals are equal."

He cannot describe his dream to them, "a dream of the earth as it will be when Man has vanished." But he does teach them an old animal song, "Beasts of England," which came back to him in his dream. The repeated singing of this revolutionary song throws the animals into a frenzy.

Major dies soon after, but the animals feel they should prepare for the Rebellion he preached. The work of teaching and organizing the others falls on the pigs, thought to be the cleverest animals. Snow-ball and Napoleon are "pre-eminent among the pigs"; and then there is Squealer, "a brilliant talker."

Mr. Jones drinks and neglects his farm more and more. One evening, when he has forgotten to feed them for over a day, the animals break into the store-shed and begin helping themselves. Jones and his men charge in, lashing with their whips. This is more than the hungry animals can bear. They all fling themselves on their tormentors. The surprised and frightened men are driven from the farm. Unexpectedly, the Rebellion has been accomplished. Jones is expelled; Manor Farm belongs to the animals.

The joy of the animals knows no bounds when they realize that they're now the owners of the farm they've worked on all their lives. They're enthusiastic when the pigs, who have taught themselves to read and write, change the sign MANOR FARM to ANIMAL FARM, and paint the Seven Commandments of Animalism on the barn wall:

1. Whatever goes upon two legs is an enemy.

2. Whatever goes upon four legs, or has wings, is a friend.

3. No animal shall wear clothes.

4. No animal shall sleep in a bed.

5. No animal shall drink alcohol.

6. No animal shall kill any other animal.

7. All animals are equal.

Now the cows must be milked. The pigs manage to do this. "What is going to happen to all that milk?" says someone. "Never mind the milk, comrade," cries

Napoleon. "The main thing is to get the harvest in."
When they come back from the fields, the milk has
disappeared.

Despite the newness of running the farm by themselves, the animals succeed in doing all tasks in record
time. The pigs' cleverness, everyone's enthusiasm,
and hard work—especially the work of Boxer, the
huge cart-horse—pull them through.

On Sundays there are ceremonies to celebrate the
Rebellion, and meetings to plan work. (Here, Snowball and Napoleon never seem to agree.) The animals
are taught to read, but the dumber ones can't even
learn the Seven Commandments, so Snowball reduces them all to one maxim: FOUR LEGS GOOD,
TWO LEGS BAD. The sheep like to bleat it for hours
on end. Snowball also organizes Committees, but
Napoleon is not interested; he's concerned with the
education of the young, and takes two litters of puppies away as soon as they're weaned, saying he'll
educate them. As for the missing milk, it goes to the
pigs, as do the new apples. Squealer explains that this
is absolutely necessary for all the brainwork the pigs
do; otherwise Jones might come back, and nobody
wants that to happen.

Jones and his men do try to retake the farm. But
Snowball has prepared the animals, and thanks to his
cleverness   and   courage—and   Boxer's   great
strength—they fight off the invaders.

There is growing conflict between Snowball and
Napoleon. Snowball comes up with the idea of a
grand project: building a windmill; Napoleon says it
will come to nothing. Snowball says they should stir
animals to rebel on other farms; Napoleon says they
should get guns for their own. Finally, when Snowball concludes an eloquent speech about labor-saving

electricity to be produced by the windmill, Napoleon gives a signal. Then nine huge dogs—the pups he had raised—bound in and charge at Snowball, who barely escapes from the farm with his life.

Napoleon, surrounded by his fierce dogs, announces that there will be no more time-wasting debates: a special Committee of pigs, chaired by himself, will simply give the animals their work orders each week. Four young pigs begin to protest, but growls from the dogs silence them, and the sheep bleat FOUR LEGS GOOD, TWO LEGS BAD over and over, preventing discussion.

Surprisingly, a few days later Napoleon announces that the windmill will be built after all. The animals slave and sacrifice for the project. Some of their food has to be sold to buy building materials. The pigs, however, have moved into the farmhouse, where they sleep in beds. This is absolutely necessary, says Squealer. But isn't it contrary to the Fourth Commandment? The animals check: "No animal shall sleep in a bed *with sheets*," it says. Meanwhile a storm topples the half-built windmill. Napoleon blames the destruction on Snowball.

In fact, although Boxer refuses to believe Snowball was a traitor from the start, there seem to be signs of Snowball's sabotage all over when things go wrong. One day, Napoleon orders all animals to assemble in the yard. The dogs rush forward and grab four young pigs by the ear and drag them before Napoleon. (They also rush at Boxer, but he simply pins one to the ground and lets him go.) The terrified pigs confess they were in league with Snowball to destroy the windmill and hand the Farm over to Man. After they confess, the dogs tear their throats out. The same thing happens to three hens, a goose, etc. The confessions pile up and so do the corpses. The depressed, frightened animals creep away when the executions are over.

Some of the animals think they remember that these killings violate the Sixth Commandment. But on the barn wall they read: "No animal shall kill any other animal *without cause.*" Later, still more animals are executed for conspiring to kill Napoleon. He is now constantly surrounded by dogs, and showered with honors: for example, a poem to his glory is inscribed on the barn wall.

Animal Farm is attacked by its neighbor, Mr. Frederick, and his armed men; the men take possession of the whole pasture, and blow up the windmill. But after a bitter fight, the animals repel the invaders, though some animals are killed and almost all are wounded. The pigs celebrate with a drinking party.

Soon after, there's a mysterious crash one night. Squealer is found on the ground next to a ladder at the barn wall, with a pot of paint near him. A few days later, the animals notice there's another commandment they had remembered wrong: it reads "No animal shall drink alcohol *to excess.*"

Times are hard, rations short for everyone (except for the pigs, who need their food), the windmill must be rebuilt, and a schoolhouse built for the young pigs. Boxer works tirelessly, although he is getting old. He wants to lay up a good store of building stone before he retires. One day as he's pulling a cartload, he collapses. Squealer announces that Comrade Napoleon is making special arrangements to have Boxer treated at a nearby hospital. When the van comes to take him away, however, his friend Benjamin the donkey reads the sign on its side: in fact, he discovers, they're taking Boxer to the horse slaughterer. But it's too late; the van drives away. Three days later, Squealer paints a moving picture of Boxer's death in the hospital. The pigs will hold a banquet in his honor, he says. There is raucous singing in the farmhouse that night; somewhere the pigs have acquired the money to buy another case of whiskey.

Years pass. The animals work hard and often go hungry. There are many new buildings and machines on the farm, and also many new dogs and pigs. Maybe this is why the animals have no more to eat than before. But at least it's their farm.

One day Squealer takes the sheep to a secluded spot for a whole week. When they return, the animals see something strange and frightening: a pig walking on its hind legs. Yes, first Squealer, then the other pigs, walk upright out of the farmhouse. Finally Napoleon himself appears. He is carrying a whip in his trotter (foot). The animals are perhaps about to protest—when all the sheep burst out into a bleating of FOUR LEGS GOOD, TWO LEGS BETTER!—and the pigs file back into the house. Clover the mare asks Benjamin to read the Commandments to her, and he does. All that's left on the wall is one slogan:

ALL ANIMALS ARE EQUAL,
BUT SOME ANIMALS ARE MORE EQUAL THAN
OTHERS.

From then on, the pigs all carry whips; they buy a radio, dress in Jones' clothes. Soon they receive a visit from neighboring farmers. Loud voices and song are heard coming from the farmhouse that night. Despite their fear, the animals are curious; they creep up to the windows to watch. Men and pigs are sitting around the table, drinking and speech-making. When a farmer toasts the success of Animal Farm—its discipline and enforced work leave nothing to be desired by any standard—Napoleon replies that he will take some more measures to cement normal business relations with their neighbors: the custom of animals addressing one another as "comrade" will be abolished, for example (singing "Beasts of England" had been forbidden long ago) and the farm will go back to its original name: Manor Farm. But the party soon degenerates into a quarrel. When the animals peek in again, they find that as they look from pig to man, from man to pig, it is impossible to say which is which.

The Characters

In *Animal Farm* Orwell is more concerned with political psychology than with individual characters. Remember, this is a *fable*, not a novel. The animals are meant to represent certain *types* of human beings, not complex individuals. Some of them are even group characters, without any individual name: "the sheep," "the hens." The "main character" of *Animal Farm* is actually *all* of the animals taken together as a group. It's what happens to the group as a whole—whether their Rebellion succeeds or fails, and why—that really matters. Still, it is important to notice the distinctions between certain types and individuals.

THE PIGS

They lead the Rebellion from the start and progressively take on the same power and characteristics as the human masters they helped overthrow. They represent corrupted human leaders, in particular, the Bolsheviks, who led the overthrow of the capitalist Russian government, only to become new masters in their turn.

Old Major

Old Major is the wise old pig whose stirring speech to the animals helps set the Rebellion in motion—though he dies before it actually begins. His role compares with that of Karl Marx, whose ideas set the Communist Revolution in motion.

Napoleon and Snowball

Napoleon and Snowball struggle for leadership of the Farm after Major's death. Snowball is an energetic, brilliant leader. He's the one who successfully organizes the defense of the Farm (like Trotsky with the Red Army). He's an eloquent speaker with original—although not necessarily beneficial—ideas (the windmill). Napoleon is a "large, rather fierce-looking Berkshire boar, not much of a talker, but with a reputation for getting his own way." And so he does. Instead of debating with Snowball, he sets his dogs on him and continues to increase his personal power and privileges from that time on. What counts for him is *power*, not ideas. Note his name: think of the other Napoleon (Bonaparte) who took over the French Revolution and turned it into a personal Empire. Napoleon's character also suggests that of Stalin and other dictators as well.

Squealer

Squealer is short, fat, twinkle-eyed and nimble, "a brilliant talker." He has a way of skipping from side to side and whisking his tail that is somehow very persuasive. They say he can turn black into white! That's just what he does, again and again: every time the pigs take more wealth and power, Squealer persuades the animals that this is absolutely necessary for the well-being of all. When things are scarce, he proves that production has increased—with figures. He is also the one who makes all the changes in the Seven Commandments. In human terms he is the propaganda apparatus that spreads the "big lie" and makes people believe in it.

THE HORSES

Boxer and Clover

Boxer and Clover represent the long-suffering workers and peasants of the world. Orwell presents them as being big, strong, patient, and decent—but not too bright. Boxer believes in the Rebellion and in its Leader. His two favorite sayings are "Napoleon is always right" and "I will work harder." His huge size and strength and his untiring labor save the Farm again and again. He finally collapses from age and overwork, and is sold for glue. Clover the mare is a motherly, protective figure. She survives to experience, dimly and wordlessly, all the sadness of the failed Revolution.

Mollie

Mollie, the frivolous, luxury-loving mare, contrasts with Clover. She deserts Animal Farm for sugar and ribbons at a human inn. Orwell may have been thinking of certain Russian nobles who left after the Revolution, or of a general human type.

OTHER ANIMALS

The Dogs

The dogs represent the means used by a totalitarian state to terrorize its own people. Think of them as Napoleon's secret police.

The Sheep

The stupid sheep keep bleating away any slogan the pigs teach them. You can guess who they are.

Muriel

Muriel the goat reads better than Clover and often reads things (such as Commandments) out loud to her.

Benjamin

Gloomy Benjamin, the donkey, may remind you of Eeyore in *Winnie-the-Pooh*, except that unlike Eeyore he never complains about his own personal problems.

He is a skeptic and a pessimist—we'd almost say a cynic, if it weren't for his loyal devotion to Boxer. Like his friend, he doesn't talk much and patiently does his work, although—unlike Boxer—no more than is required. He's also unlike Boxer in that he does not believe in the Revolution, nor in anything else, except that life is hard. Whatever political question he is asked, he replies only that "Donkeys live a long time" and "None of you has ever seen a dead donkey." He survives.

The Pigeons

The pigeons spread the word of Rebellion beyond the farm, as many Communists spread the doctrine of the revolution beyond the boundaries of the Soviet Union.

Moses

Moses the Raven, who does no work, but tells comforting tales of the wonderful Sugarcandy Mountain where you go when you die, is a satire of organized religion. (Marx called religion, in a famous phrase, "the opiate of the people.") In terms of Russia, Moses represents the Orthodox Church. Watch what happens to him in the story.

THE HUMANS

Farmer Jones

In the narrowest sense the drunken, negligent Farmer Jones represents the Czar. He also stands for any government that declines through its own corruption and mismanagement.

Pilkington

Pilkington, who likes hunting and fishing more than farming, represents Orwell's view of the decadent British gentleman in particular—and of the Allied nations in general, especially Britain and France.

Frederick

The cruel Frederick represents Germany.

Whymper

Whymper is a commercial go-between for animals and humans—just as certain capitalists have always transacted business with Communist nations.

Other Elements

SETTING

As its title implies, *Animal Farm* is set on a farm. But Orwell uses the farm to represent a universe in miniature. It sometimes seems idyllic, peaceful, fresh, spring-like. Usually moments when it is perceived in this way contrast ironically with the real situation of the animals. The setting suggests an attitude: "this could be utopia, but . . ." It does not really interest Orwell in itself. Sometimes he sketches a wintry, bleak, cold decor, a perfect backdrop for hard times. Here you could think of the setting as a metaphor—a way of representing hard times.

THEME

Animal Farm concerns one of the central political experiences of our time: revolution.

On those relatively rare occasions when men and women have decided to change radically the system of government they were born under, there has been revolution. It has been on the rise in the last three hundred years of human history. If we want to understand the world we live in, we must try to understand the phenomenon of revolution—the how, the why, the what-happens-then. One way of doing so is to see how an imaginative writer deals with it. You can think of this as an important benefit of reading *Animal Farm*.

Animal Farm is also about another crucial political phenomenon of our time, one which is perhaps unique to the 20th century: the rise of the totalitarian state. Even though he's less concerned with totalitarianism in *Animal Farm* than in his novel *1984*, Orwell does give us an imaginative analysis of totalitarian dictatorship in *Animal Farm*. So another thing we can get from this book is a feel for how a modern dictatorship works.

STYLE

The story of *Animal Farm* is told in a simple, straightforward style. The sentences are often short and spare, with a simple subject-verb-object structure: "Old Major cleared his throat and began to sing." "It was a bitter winter."

The story follows a single line of action, calmly told, with no digressions. Orwell's style, said one critic, has the "relentless simplicity" and "pathetic doggedness" of the animals themselves. There is a kind of tension in *Animal Farm* between the sad story the author has to tell and the lucid, almost light way he tells it.

POINT OF VIEW

Orwell uses point of view in *Animal Farm* to create *irony*. Irony is a contrast or contradiction, such as between what a statement seems to say and what it really means—or between what characters expect to happen and what really happens. The story is told from the naïve point of view of the lower animals, not from that of the clever pigs or an all-seeing narrator. Thus, when there's a crash one night and Squealer is found in the barn sprawled on the ground beside a broken ladder, a brush, and a pot of paint, it is "a strange incident which hardly anyone was able to understand." A few days later the animals find that the Fifth Commandment painted on the barn wall is not exactly as they remembered it; in fact there are, they can now see, two words at the end that "they had forgotten." No comment from the narrator.

This simple irony is sometimes charged with great intensity in *Animal Farm*. For example, when Boxer, who has literally worked himself to death for the Farm, is carted off in a van to the "hospital," and Benjamin reads out "Horse Slaughterer" on the side of the van (too late), we know—and for once at least some of the animals know—what has really happened: the sick horse has been sold for glue. No irony. But when Squealer gives his fake explanation about the vet who didn't have time to paint over the slaughterer's old sign, we are gravely informed that "The animals were enormously relieved to hear this." And two paragraphs later, at the end of the chapter, when there is a banquet—for the pigs—in Boxer's honor, we hear the sound of singing coming from the farmhouse, and the last sentence tells us that the word went round that from somewhere or other the pigs had acquired the money to buy themselves another case of whisky." Most of the animals don't make the connection between Boxer's being taken away and the pigs suddenly having more money—and the narrator doesn't *seem* to make the connection either. But Orwell makes sure we, the readers, don't miss it. The irony—the contrast between what the animals believe, what the narrator actually tells us, and what we *know* to be the truth—fills us with more anger than an open denunciation could have done.

FORM AND STRUCTURE

Animal Farm successfully combines the characteristics of three literary forms—the fable, the satire, and the allegory.

Animal Farm is a fable—a story usually having a moral, in which beasts talk and act like men and women. Orwell's animal characters are both animal and human. The pigs, for example, eat mash—real pig food—but with milk in it that they have grabbed and persuaded the other animals to let them keep (a human action). The dogs growl and bite the way real dogs do—but to support Napoleon's drive for political power. Orwell never forgets this delicate balance between how real animals actually behave and what human qualities his animals are supposed to represent.

Part of the fable's humorous charm lies in the simplicity with which the characters are drawn. Each animal character is a type, with one human trait, or two at most—traits usually associated with that particular kind of animal. Using animals as types is also Orwell's way of keeping his hatred and anger against exploiters under control. Instead of crying, "All political bosses are vicious pigs!" he keeps his sense of humor by reporting calmly: "In future, all questions relating to the working of the farm would be settled by a special committee of pigs." (No wonder that when a publisher who rejected the book, afraid to give offense, wanted to have some animal other than pigs representing these bosses, Orwell called it an "imbecile suggestion.")

The aspect of human life that most interested Orwell was not psychological; it was political: how people act as a group, how societies are formed and function. Clearly, *Animal Farm* is a story about a revolution for an ideal, and about how that ideal is increasingly betrayed until it disappears altogether from the new society after the revolution. Since Orwell attacks that new society, and since, despite the grim, bitter picture he paints of it, he attacks it with humor (the humor of the beast fable), we can also call *Animal Farm* a satire.

The immediate object of attack in Orwell's political satire is the society that was created in Russia after the Bolshevik Revolution of 1917. The events narrated in *Animal Farm* obviously and continuously refer to events in another story, the history of the Russian Revolution. In other words, *Animal Farm* is not only a charming fable ("A Fairy Story," as Orwell playfully subtitles it) and a bitter political satire; it is also an allegory.

You can enjoy *Animal Farm* without knowing this, of course, just as you can enjoy Swift's *Gulliver's Travels* without realizing that it, too, is a bitter satire and in places a political allegory. But to understand the book as fully as possible, we'll want to pay attention to the historical allegory as we go along.

The Story
CHAPTER I

Because *Animal Farm* is a story about a revolution betrayed, and Orwell wants us to feel how terrible this betrayal is, he knows it's important for us to begin by feeling the force of the hopes and ideals the Revolution started out with. This is what he tries to convey in the two opening chapters. He also suggests, subtly at first, and then more sharply, what kinds of things will lead to the betrayal of the revolutionary ideal. But the opening isn't too serious or heavy-handed; it is here above all that Orwell works with the conciseness, simplicity, and concrete detail that give his story humor and charm. He wants us to know it's the beginning of a fable: we can immediately be amused by watching characters who are both animals and people at the same time. It's also the beginning of the Revolution, so the atmosphere is mostly hopeful—although we can see dark shadows underneath if we look.

Chapter I describes a revolutionary meeting. This chapter 1. sets the scene: the drunken farmer and all the farm animals; 2. sets up the situation: the revolutionary vision, in Major's speech and song, sets the animals on fire; 3. suggests problems for the future.

It's easy to imagine an old joke, or cartoon, beginning just about the way *Animal Farm* does: When Farmer Jones comes home drunk one night . . . Then the snoring wife, the light out in the bedroom, AND THEN in the semidarkness, the animals gathering to hear a speech. The visual effects of the first paragraph are as clear as a cartoon: "With the ring of light from his lantern dancing from side to side, he lurched across the yard." The character of Farmer Jones himself is like a cartoon character. Soon we'll see that his drunkenness and irresponsibility ("too drunk to remember to shut the pop-holes") will have serious consequences—and a deeper meaning. For now, note the name: "Farmer Jones" is not only a stock farmer's name in a joke. It is also a way of saying *any* farmer, the typical farmer.

As is fitting for the only chapter in the book entirely taking place on the farm when it is owned and run by Jones, the first and last paragraphs center on his actions. They provide a neat little frame for the chapter.

Now the focus turns to the animals. From the start Orwell presents them simultaneously as both animals—"there was a stirring and a fluttering all through the farm buildings"—and as characters who talk and react as human beings—"*Word* had gone round . . ." that Major "had a strange dream . . . and wished to communicate it to the other animals. It had been agreed . . ." Their human situation is already one of resistance to a dangerous master—"they should all meet in the big barn as soon as Mr. Jones was safely out of the way." But they have a "highly regarded" leader in Old Major. Since "everyone was quite ready to lose an hour's sleep to hear what he had to say," we realize that an important speech is about to be made.

First Orwell introduces us to the speaker and his audience. The leader is already comfortably in place "on his bed of straw" (animal again), "under a lantern which hung from a beam" (this convincing human detail is a cartoon touch if ever there was one). Then, one by one, as they come into the barn, we are introduced to all the main characters and the rest of the farm animals.

NOTE: Throughout this introduction, there is a pleasant humor in the way the combinations of human and animal traits are described. Even though they're about to listen to a speech and have clearly human traits (middle-aged Clover "had never quite got her figure back after her fourth foal," Benjamin is known for his cynical remarks, "foolish pretty" Mollie hopes to draw attention to her ribbons), each is a different kind of animal, and Orwell never lets us forget it: "the hens perched themselves on the windowsills, the pigeons fluttered up to the rafters, the sheep and cows lay down . . . and began to chew the cud." And they are true to their nature: "Last of all came the cat, who looked round, as usual, for the warmest places, and finally squeezed herself in between Boxer and Clover; there she purred contentedly throughout Major's speech without listening to a word of what he was saying."

As we consider all these types and classes of "people," quick and slow, large and small, bright and dumb, we can't help thinking of them as a whole society, complete in itself. Before he begins to talk, Major, like any speaker with presence and authority, makes sure all the animals are "waiting attentively." So are we. When he clears his throat and begins, we know we're in for the main event.

"Comrades," he begins—and this is the first hint of political allegory in the tale: "Comrade" has been the term of address among socialist revolutionaries for almost a century. It still is common in the Soviet Union. So there is already a hint that this story about a farm is really about revolutionary politics. Not that Major is going to talk about politics in the usual American sense of the word. Before telling his dream, he's going to speak to them, with all the benefit of his age and experience, about "the nature of life."

Major paints a grim picture of the "natural" life of animals. He soon makes them realize, however, that what seems natural isn't: animals are miserable, hungry slaves because man enslaves them, profits from their labor, and gives them in return just barely enough to stay alive. In other words, what seems a philosophical question ("the nature of life") is really a political problem (who has power over whom? who profits from whom?). Since it's a political problem, it has a political solution: get rid of the enslaver, get rid of Man.

In the first paragraph, Major begins skillfully setting up this solution by at first using passive forms to show the misery of the animal condition without saying who is responsible: "we are given just so much food as will keep the breath in our bodies," "[we] are forced to work to the last atom of our strength." A born orator, he drives home his point with repetition and short, simple, generalizing phrases: "No animal in England knows the meaning of happiness or leisure after he is a year old. No animal in England is free. The life of an animal is misery and slavery: that is the plain truth."

NOTE: There is a little joke in Major's portrait of the animal condition. When he calls their lives "miserable, laborious and short," he echoes the 17th-century thinker Thomas Hobbes' famous description of Man's life in a state of nature: "nasty, brutish, and short." Since Major is talking of animal life in a given political situation—subjection to Man—the phrase comes out as comical parody. You'll see that there's much more parody in Major's speech.

In the next paragraph he shows that it doesn't have
to be this way; it is not "part of the order of nature";
the land is more than rich enough to feed everybody
plentifully. Then, and only then, does Major name
the cause of the animals' misery: Man

Man takes everything from the animals and gives
them back next to nothing. Using a powerful oratori-
cal trick, Major then addresses members of his audience directly:

> "You cows that I see before me, how many thou-
> sands of gallons of milk have you given during this
> last year? And what has happened to that milk
> which should have been breeding up sturdy
> calves? Every drop of it has gone down the throats
> of our enemies. And you hens, how many eggs
> have you laid this last year, and how many of
> those eggs ever hatched into chickens? . . . And
> you, Clover, where are those four foals you bore,
> who should have been the support and pleasure
> of your old age? Each was sold at a year old . . ."

And as soon as Man can take nothing more from
them, they are "slaughtered with hideous cruelty," as
he said at the start of his speech. Now Major makes
each of them feel it:

> "You young porkers who are sitting in front of me,
> every one of you will scream your lives out at the
> block within a year. To that horror we all must
> come—cows, pigs, hens, sheep, everyone . . .
> You, Boxer, the very day that those great muscles
> of yours lose their power, Jones will sell you to the
> knacker, who will cut your throat and boil you
> down for the foxhounds."

Major accuses Man of exploitation and cruelty. In
his view there is only one way out: "get rid of Man"—
and only one way to do it: "Rebellion!" Only when
the Rebellion occurs—and it may not come for gener-
ations, he says—will the animals "become rich and

free." As a matter of fact, the Rebellion will triumph in the very next chapter. We'll see what becomes of the two themes of exploitation and cruelty when Man is removed and the animals run the farm by themselves. Keep your eyes particularly on Major's last example: the fate of Boxer.

For now, Major tells them, they must unite against the common enemy: "All animals are comrades." Unfortunately, he is interrupted at this very moment by the uproar of the dogs chasing the rats, who barely escape with their lives. Major sees the problem:

> "Comrades," he said, "here is a point that must be settled. The wild creatures, such as rats and rabbits—are they our friends or our enemies? Let us put it to the vote. I propose this question to the meeting: Are rats comrades?"

They vote rats as comrades, with only four dissenters: "the three dogs, and the cat, who was afterwards discovered to have voted on both sides."

Now at this point, most of us will be grinning from ear to ear, if we're not laughing out loud. What had seemed a moving speech has turned into comedy. The joke comes from the contradiction of Major's ideal pronouncement "All animals are comrades" with animal reality: dogs and cats kill rats. The animals' majority vote—the democratic ideal—is not about to change that. We'll come back to this question of ideal vision versus real nature later.

The other source of humor here is Major's utterly human political vocabulary ("put it to the vote," "propose this question to the meeting"). We realize, if we haven't done so earlier, that we can't quite listen to Major's speech as an animal's denunciation of human cruelty to animals. It is also a human speech about man's cruelty to man. The fable is also an allegory: it stands for another story, which deepens its meaning.

And this allegorical speech is also a parody, which amuses us once we realize what it refers to: just as Major is—humorously—both pig and human, his speech is—again, humorously—both his and that of a human revolutionary idealist: Karl Marx.

Major's speech is a summary, in animal terms, of the socialist view of the human condition, particularly as described by Marx. Workers and peasants (the proletariat) labor for the profit of the owners of the means of production (the bourgeoisie). From the work of the proletariat, the owners gain wealth and money for investment (capital); in return, Marx said, they give the workers back just enough money to stay alive, in the form of wages. (Remember, Marx was writing in the middle of the 19th century, when wages were very low and working hours very long. But Orwell, too, had seen terrible working-class conditions in the English mining country.)

The condition of the animals under Man, in Major's speech, is the condition of the proletariat under the bourgeoisie as the socialists traditionally saw it. And the solution is the same. As Marx and Engels wrote in the famous closing lines of the *Communist Manifesto*: "Let the ruling classes tremble at a Communist revolution. The proletarians have nothing to lose but their chains. They have a world to win. WORKING MEN OF ALL COUNTRIES UNITE!"

NOTE: You can read Major's speech without thinking of Marx, just as you can read the rest of *Animal Farm* without thinking of the Soviet Union. But would it still be funny? Perhaps it would still have the humor of a fable—the very fact of a revolutionary speaker addressing members of the crowd as "You hens . . ." is enough to raise a smile. Knowing Marx—in other

words, making the Animal Meeting an allegory
and Major's speech a parody—makes the story both
deeper and funnier. Deeper, because we may feel, as
the socialist Orwell certainly did, the passion for justice that stirs the animals. Funnier, because it's amus-
ing to discover Marx's ideas in the animal's com-
plaints.

Major goes on to summarize the animals' "duty of
enmity towards Man":

> "Whatever goes upon two legs, is an enemy.
> Whatever goes upon four legs, or has wings, is a
> friend. And remember also that in fighting against
> Man, we must not come to resemble him."

From this basic principle, Major draws his essential
commandments:

> "No animal must ever live in a house, or sleep in a
> bed, or wear clothes, or drink alcohol, or smoke
> tobacco, or touch money, or engage in trade."

"And, above all," he says, the doctrine of animal solidarity and equality should characterize the struggle
and the new society after the Revolution:

> ". . . no animal must ever tyrannize over his own
> kind. Weak or strong, clever or simple, we are all
> brothers. No animal must ever kill any other ani-
> mal. All animals are equal."

NOTE: You may take Major's whole speech as a
mocking parody. Some readers feel that Orwell is
laughing at inflammatory revolutionists and their
gullible audience. But other readers are amused *and*
moved by Major's speech. Parody, they feel, can be
serious and funny at the same time. In the last analysis, how you react to Major's speech, and for that

matter to the "revolution" that follows, may depend on your own political feelings. Or, perhaps, those feelings will be changed by this book.

When Major comes to his indescribable dream, "a dream of the earth as it will be when Man has vanished" (in human terms, the dream of a society in which social classes have disappeared), and the song that came back to him in that dream, Orwell again introduces unmistakably humorous elements. The song is "a stirring tune," the narrator says, and then adds, "something between 'Clementine' and 'La Cucaracha.' " (And in fact the song can be sung to either of these tunes.)

In the excitement it has for the animals, in its revolutionary function, "Beasts of England" resembles songs that have actually played a role in worker uprisings around the world. And its vision—an end to inequality, cruelty, and exploitation, a victorious struggle to bring forth "the golden future time"—was Orwell's own vision when he saw revolutionary Barcelona in 1937. The writer Arthur Koestler, who knew Orwell, thought the song—particularly the last stanza—expressed Orwell's own hopes and ideals. This is all true. But just try to sing those words to the tune of "Clementine" or "La Cucaracha" without laughing!

And just in case we've forgotten that it's an animal fable, Orwell reminds us when the animals sing the song: "The cows lowed it, the dogs whined it, the sheep bleated it, the horses whinnied it, the ducks quacked it."

Then Mr. Jones's drunken shot in the dark silences the animals, and Orwell ends the first chapter with the tone of a bedtime fable: "The birds jumped on to their perches, the animals settled down in the straw, and the whole farm was asleep in a moment."

NOTE: We've already seen that there may be some problems for the animal solidarity and equality of dogs and rats, even in "the golden future time." If we look back at Orwell's presentation of Major's audience—the characters in the book—we can see that they form a kind of society in miniature, with its own distinctions, and perhaps hierarchy. For example, we may wonder why the pigs settle down "immediately in front of the platform." Boxer is "not of first rate intelligence," and he seems to work harder than the others. Mollie and the cat are not interested in Major's speech at all, although for different reasons. Whatever Orwell's intentions, the very fact that this is a fable, with the animals' role and personality defined once and for all by their kind, suggests that there is a natural order, a natural hierarchy—and natural antagonisms, too. How can revolution change that?

We do see brotherly, protective behavior on the part of the animals, though. Boxer and Clover come in "together, walking very slowly and setting down their vast hairy hoofs with great care lest there should be some small animal concealed in the straw." Then, when the motherless ducklings wander around the barn to find a safe place, "Clover made a sort of wall round them with her great foreleg, and the ducklings nestled down inside it." They perform these comradely actions before Major's speech about hatred to Man and comradeship among animals. Orwell seems to be suggesting that there is some instinctive decency in the working class.

Major's idealistic vision may be doomed by certain realities of nature: hierarchy and antagonism. Or will the society created by the Rebellion encourage the natural decency of animals like Boxer and Clover? If we look carefully, we see that Orwell has hinted at problems for the Rebellion from the very start.

CHAPTER II

The Rebellion happens. It is preceded by the animals' preparation for it and the human master's mismanagement and neglect; then there is a spontaneous revolt. Next we see the animals' joy in the victorious revolution—the farm is theirs!—and the first steps at making a new society based on animal solidarity and equality. This principle is subtly undermined throughout, however, by the increasingly dominant role played by the pigs, especially Napoleon and Snowball. Finally an incident at the very end of the chapter reveals the first clear betrayal of the revolutionary ideal.

Like many teachers and prophets, Major dies before he can see his dream realized. But it immediately has a profound effect on the way the animals see their world:

> Major's speech had given to the more intelligent animals on the farm a completely new outlook on life. They did not know when the Rebellion predicted by Major would take place, they had no reason for thinking that it would be within their own lifetime, but they saw clearly that it was their duty to prepare for it.

But our careful reading of Chapter I leads us to be alert to what follows:

> The work of teaching and organizing the others
> fell naturally upon the pigs, who were generally
> recognized as being the cleverest of the animals.

These words suggest a disturbing contradiction once
again: preparation for an egalitarian revolution is being led by those who seem to be on the top of a natural
hierarchy.

We are then introduced to the pigs—Snowball,
Napoleon, and Squealer. Part of their work has been
to elaborate old Major's "teachings" into a "complete
system of thought" they call Animalism. Major's
vision has been transformed into a doctrine. But this is
only the first transformation his ideas will undergo.

NOTE: Not all of the animals immediately accept
the doctrine of Animalism. Some of them question the
need for revolution—and are dismissed as being stupid and apathetic. Look at some of the questions the
animals raise. Do you think all of their objections are
stupid? Do you think Orwell thought they were?

We would expect Boxer and Clover, hardworking
and simple, to be the "most faithful disciples" of the
new vision. And they are: ". . . having once accepted
the pigs as their teachers, they absorbed everything
that they were told, and passed it on to the other animals by simple arguments." This quotation highlights
that unsettling contradiction once again: Boxer and
Clover are working for the Rebellion in the name of
equality, yet their position seems subordinate—
worse still, naturally subordinate—to the pigs.

As for Moses, the tame raven, we recall that he was
the only animal who didn't even come to the meeting
in the barn. He represents religion in the fable—he

encourages the animals to comfort themselves for the troubles of this life by thinking of the happiness to come in the afterlife, Sugarcandy Mountain: ". . . some of them believed in Sugarcandy Mountain, and the pigs had to argue very hard to persuade them that there was no such place." The new faith replaces the old with difficulty.

Next Orwell swiftly sketches Farmer Jones' increasing mismanagement and neglect. Finally, one day in June, Jones goes on a binge and forgets to feed the animals all day. Out of sheer hunger, they break into the storeroom and begin to help themselves. When Jones and his men charge in and start whipping them, the "Rebellion" occurs:

> With one accord, though nothing of the kind had been planned beforehand, they flung themselves upon their tormentors. Jones and his men suddenly found themselves being butted and kicked from all sides. . . . They had never seen animals behave like this before, and this sudden uprising of creatures whom they were used to thrashing and maltreating just as they chose, frightened them almost out of their wits. . . . they gave up trying to defend themselves and took to their heels.

The Rebellion is spontaneous ("nothing of the kind had been planned beforehand"), but would it have happened without Major and without the animals' preparation for it? At any rate, there is no leader; Orwell does not give the name of one single animal. For him, revolution is the affair of the people as a whole. And clearly, his sympathy is on the side of the Revolution, "this sudden uprising of creatures whom [the masters] were used to thrashing and maltreating just as they chose."

Orwell's sympathy for the rebels' joy in the victorious revolution is still more evident in the passages that follow. The animals gallop all around the farm "as though to make sure that no human being was hiding anywhere upon it"; then they race back to the farm buildings to destroy all the cruel traces of human oppression: bits, nose-rings, castrating knives, etc. "All the animals capered with joy when they saw the whips going up in flames." (Keep this detail in mind. We'll see it again later.)

Perhaps Boxer goes too far when, after hearing Snowball declare that animals should shun any form of clothes as "the mark of a human being," he burns a small hat he wore in summer to keep the flies out of his ears. And again, what may seem natural when we first read it (and what seems natural to the animals) is slightly sinister if we take a closer look: "Napoleon led them back to the store-shed and served out a double ration of corn to everybody . . ." Why does he have to lead and serve things out to them?

Still, the main intent of these passages is to make us feel the joy of those who have never owned anything when they suddenly realize they own the place they have worked in all their lives. There are scenes of joy in pure, utopian nature in a number of Orwell's other novels (particularly in *Coming Up for Air* and *1984*), but they are usually dreams or memories that contrast ironically with a soiled and dismal present. In *Animal Farm*, this passage of revolutionary joy will contrast ironically with a harsh and dismal future.

The farmhouse, symbolizing the repressive past, is turned into a museum. After burying some hams (delightful detail—why do you think they do that?), they leave the house untouched, and agree unanimously that "no animal must ever live there." And we'll see what happens to that resolution.

The pigs have taught themselves to read and write. Again a detail makes it come alive: "from an old spelling book which had belonged to Mr. Jones's children and which had been thrown on the rubbish heap." Snowball succeeds in painting out MANOR FARM from the gate and painting in ANIMAL FARM. The pigs have also "succeeded in reducing the principles of Animalism to Seven Commandments" to be inscribed on the wall: "they would form an unalterable law by which all the animals on Animal Farm must live for ever after." So Major's dream has gone from vision to doctrine to "unalterable law," painted on the wall, thus:

1. *Whatever goes upon two legs is an enemy.*
2. *Whatever goes upon four legs, or has wings, is a friend.*
3. *No animal shall wear clothes.*
4. *No animal shall sleep in a bed.*
5. *No animal shall drink alcohol.*
6. *No animal shall kill any other animal.*
7. *All animals are equal.*

The rest of *Animal Farm* is about the progressive alteration of those written laws, until nothing is left of them except the—famous—corruption of the last one. Orwell is not only concerned with the corruption of an ideal—a corruption brought about by power (as we shall see); he is also concerned with the corruption of language that goes along with it.

At this point Orwell gives us an incident that reveals this corruption of language. The cows start lowing, and the animals realize that they have to be milked immediately. "After a little thought," the pigs manage to do this, "their trotters being well adapted to this task." (Once more, some animals just seem naturally superior!) "Soon there were five buckets of frothing creamy milk at which many of the animals looked with considerable interest."

"What is going to happen to all that milk?" said someone.

"Jones used sometimes to mix some of it in our mash," said one of the hens.

"Never mind the milk, comrades!" cried Napoleon, placing himself in front of the buckets. "That will be attended to. The harvest is more important. Comrade Snowball will lead the way. I shall follow in a few minutes. Forward, comrades! The hay is waiting."

This parody of the discourse of a dishonest revolutionary leader marks the first time in *Animal Farm* that language has been used to hide something. (It is also Napoleon's first speech in the novel.) What it's hiding is personal privilege and greed:

So the animals trooped down to the hayfield to begin the harvest, and when they came back in the evening it was noticed that the milk had disappeared.

We see the leader exercising control through language—in such a way that it almost seems natural and inevitable.

For the first time, too, Orwell uses a kind of irony that he will come back to again and again—an irony inherent in the fable's point of view. The narrator tells the story from the naïve viewpoint of the mass of animals and often in the passive voice ("it was noticed that the milk had disappeared") without giving any explanation for the event. Since the reader sees the explanation clearly enough, we can say that Orwell is using the oldest ironic trick there is: feigned ignorance. The effect on most readers is somewhere between a smile and a wince.

NOTE: You have probably begun to suspect that *Animal Farm* is a story that raises a variety of questions, a story that has meaning on many levels. The incident of the milk raises a series of interrelated problems. Let's separate them for convenience:

1. *language:* Napoleon's speech and its effect; Orwell's way of narrating the incident

2. *power:* How do the pigs get the milk? (See Chapter III for the rest of the story.)

3. *the ideal* (generous solidarity) *versus the real* (the weaknesses of "human nature," which the animals represent): Why did the pigs get the milk?

4. *the elite and the mass*

All these problems will come up again and again.

CHAPTER III

The first paragraph sets the tone and suggests the topic of this chapter:

> How they toiled and sweated to get the hay in! But their efforts were rewarded, for the harvest was an even bigger success than they had hoped.

In the early days of the Revolution, there is hard going for everyone, but the system actually works better than before, because of the animal's feelings of pride and solidarity. The result of this hard work—now that the animals own the farm—is happiness, both physical and spiritual.

However, this pleasure in the first accomplishments of the Revolution is undercut—for the reader if not for the animals—by the growing political power of the pigs. The conditions of their life are different from those of the other animals. Fittingly, the chapter ends with a full-length explanation of the "mystery of the milk"—and with apples thrown in for good measure.

We'll want to pay careful attention to Orwell's irony as he undercuts his triumphant revolutionary tale by simultaneously narrating the rise of the pigs.

Animal Farm has sometimes been read as a fable against socialism. Yet here Orwell seems to be suggesting that socialism—true socialism, in which the means of production really are owned by those who work them—is efficient and leads to happiness.

Early in the chapter, we come upon these revealing sentences, numbered here for convenience with key words in italics:

> 1. the pigs were so *clever* that they could think of a way round every difficulty. 2. As for the horses, they *knew every inch of the field,* and in fact *understood the business* of mowing and raking *better* than Jones and his men ever had done. 3. The pigs did not actually work, but directed and supervised the others. 4. With *their superior knowledge* it was *natural* that they should assume the leadership.

We have seen that the question of what is "natural" (equality or hierarchy) is constantly implied in *Animal Farm.* Here the pigs assume a superior, nonworking, managerial position because of their "natural" cleverness and knowledge. This is stated in sentences 1, 3, and 4. But where is the evidence of their knowledge? The only place we see real knowledge shown is in sentence 2, which shows the skill and knowledge of the supposedly stupid horses. It is, perhaps, "natural" to the other animals that the pigs just give orders—and it certainly seems natural to the pigs. Orwell makes no comment on this, but gives us evidence to see differently. This is typical of the irony that derives from the fable's point of view.

Where the pigs are really outstandingly clever is in political life. For example, they know how to use symbols: Snowball explains the new flag they've made, green for the green fields of England, hoof-and-horn for the Republic of Animals. (Need we recall that the Soviets made their flag hammer-and-sickle for worker-and-peasant, red for the traditional color of revolution?) They also know how to dominate the Meetings, where "the work of the coming week was planned out and resolutions were put forward and debated." The description of the Meetings contains one of the saddest sentences in this part of *Animal Farm*: "The other animals understood how to vote, but could never think of any resolutions of their own." Alas, the pigs are natural leaders. Most of the animals—like most people—are not.

Snowball's talent for organizing Animal Committees, however, runs into problems. The "Wild Comrades Re-education Committee" is a total failure, as is the cat's attempt to convince a sparrow that they are comrades: language can't always change human nature (or let's just say nature).

In the pigs' reading and writing program, we do see a natural hierarchy. But the pigs are not necessarily at the very top. Benjamin the mule, for example, can read perfectly, but doesn't: "nothing worth reading," he says. Boxer, on the other hand, can only trace out a few letters. And the sheep, hens, and ducks can't even learn the Seven Commandments, so the ingenious Snowball finds a way to reduce them to a single saying: FOUR LEGS GOOD, TWO LEGS BAD, which the sheep enjoy bleating for hours on end.

NOTE: The combination of the pigs' cleverness and the natural stupidity of some animals has caused Major's teachings to undergo still another modification. They have gone from vision to doctrine (Animalism) to "unalterable law" (the Seven Commandments) and now to slogan. Snowball claims that the slogan expresses "the essential principle of Animalism." Does it? Read the Commandments again. Can they all be fully expressed by the slogan?

Napoleon takes no interest in Snowball's committees, but goes in for "the education of the young," taking nine new puppies off to be educated. This is part of the opposition, already noted at meetings, between Napoleon and Snowball. It is also another innocent detail that becomes sinister once we've read Chapter V.

All the animals—but Boxer above all—have been straining and working tirelessly, though happily, for the welfare of the Farm. The pigs have been directing, reading, debating. Toward the end of the chapter, with no comment, and without any apparent connection to what follows, Orwell relates, as if it were another natural event: "The mystery of where the milk went to was soon cleared up. It was mixed into the pigs' mash." Moreover, when there are new apples, "The animals had assumed as a matter of course that these would be shared out equally; one day, however, "the order went forth that" they were to be brought to the pigs.

Differences in roles have led to differences in diet, to inequality and privilege. Notice how clever Orwell has been in slipping these things in. "The order went forth"—this is the first we hear of the pigs' actually issuing directives—and neither the sentence nor the animals are stopped short by the fact. Some animals may "murmur" at this particular order, "but it was no use." Again, no explanation to the reader, no analysis, just statement of the bare, inescapable fact. "All the pigs were in full agreement on this point, even Snowball and Napoleon." As if this explains why "it was no use"!

NOTE: Some readers have seen Snowball as a good, generous leader, from whose future downfall all evils will come. Given his participation in the order about the milk, would you agree?

The pigs send their mouthpiece, Squealer, to explain the decision (not to debate it, we note) to the animals. This is the first time we see him in action. In a heavy parody of hypocritical, self-seeking propaganda, Squealer tells them that many of the pigs are taking milk and apples against their wills:

> "Our sole object in taking these things is to preserve our health. Milk and apples (this has been proved by Science, comrades) contain substances absolutely necessary to the well-being of a pig. We pigs are brain-workers . . . Day and night we are watching over your welfare. It is for *your* sake that we drink that milk and eat those apples."

As a clincher, he informs them that "if we pigs failed in our duty, Jones would come back! . . . surely there is no one among you who wants to see Jones come back?" No one notices the lack of logical connection between the apples and the return of Jones. But "if there was one thing the animals were completely certain of . . . it was that they did not want Jones back." No one has any more to say.

NOTE: In a further perversion of language and the egalitarian ideal, revolutionary rhetoric has been used for obvious self-interest—obvious to the reader, that is, not the animals. Orwell's heaviest irony—it becomes sarcastic parody here—falls on propaganda, especially when propaganda works.

CHAPTER IV

After the revolutionary enthusiasm—and the increasing irony—of Chapter III, and before the grim ironies in store for us in Chapter V, the narrative in this chapter is fast and light. With the help of his men and two neighbors, Jones tries to take the farm back by force. But Snowball, who has been reading up on Caesar's campaigns, has prepared the animals to defend themselves. They defeat their former master, but not before a sheep is killed and Snowball, who has flung himself right at Mr. Jones, is injured.

As described by Orwell, the "heroic" battle is reduced to a farce, with pigeons releasing their droppings on the men's heads and geese pecking the men's legs. There is one serious and revealing incident, though. Boxer, who has been the animals' main fighter, believes he has killed a stable-boy (or so he thinks). It was unintentional, he says sorrowfully.

> "No sentimentality, comrade!" cried Snowball, from whose wounds the blood was still dripping. "War is war. The only good human being is a dead one."
> "I have no wish to take life, not even human life," repeated Boxer, and his eyes were full of tears.

Orwell's point is that leaders stick to the political goal, regardless of the means needed to attain it. Ordinary people, on the other hand, confronted with a real, individual human death, have more decency.

But the stable-boy is not dead after all; he gets up and runs away while the animals are searching for Mollie, who had taken flight when the farmer's gun went off. And the chapter ends when the animals decorate Snowball and Boxer "Animal Hero, First Class," name their victory the "Battle of the Cowshed," and decide to celebrate it every year.

Orwell wants to keep things light in this chapter. Yet the Battle of the Cowshed allegorically tells the story of the Russian Civil War. Why Orwell wished to treat this terrible war in this way is open to question.

CHAPTER V

This chapter begins lightly enough. Clover has seen the frivolous, lazy Mollie talking to a human being and "allowing him to stroke your nose." Mollie's reaction to the accusation is pure comedy:

> "He didn't! I wasn't! It isn't true!" cried Mollie, beginning to prance about and paw the ground.

Except for the horselike gestures, she behaves like an accused child. Soon after, she deserts the Farm for a human master who gives her sugar and ribbons. "She appeared to be enjoying herself," say the pigeons who spotted her. They never mention Mollie again.

NOTE: We may wonder what this episode about Mollie has to do with the rest of the chapter, which deals with the growing conflict between Snowball and Napoleon, Snowball's expulsion from the Farm, and

Napoleon's consolidation of personal power by means of his terrifying dogs. Perhaps Orwell is suggesting that Mollie got out while the getting was good.

During a winter of "bitterly hard weather" the Farm has moved one little step further along the road to inequality: "It had come to be accepted that the pigs, who were manifestly cleverer than the other animals, should decide all questions of farm policy, though their decisions had to be ratified by a majority vote." Once again the narrator presents us with an accomplished fact.

Unfortunately, in reaching these decisions, Snowball and Napoleon clash about absolutely everything. Each shows a distinct political personality in the struggle:

> At the Meetings Snowball often won over the majority by his brilliant speeches, but Napoleon was better at canvassing support for himself in between times.

Napoleon, the narrator tells us, is particularly good at getting the sheep to start bleating "Four legs good, two legs bad" at key points in Snowball's speeches. You see how Orwell feels about members of the Communist Party who supported Stalin as he rose. But do Snowball's schemes, which he devises from reading some old agriculture magazines lying around the house, come off much better?

> He talked learnedly about field-drains, silage, and basic slag, and had worked out a complicated scheme for all the animals to drop their dung directly in the fields, at a different spot every day, to save the labor of cartage.

The main issue between the two pigs is the great windmill project. Using old do-it-yourself books he found, Snowball has concocted a vast plan to build a windmill that would supply the Farm with free electricity. This in turn could operate farm machines. Napoleon, who "produced no schemes of his own, but said quietly that Snowball's would come to nothing, and seemed to be biding his time," opposes the idea. The other animals admire Snowball's complicated drawings. As for Napoleon, who comes to examine them one day,

> He walked heavily round the shed, looked closely at every detail of the plans and snuffed at them once or twice, then stood for a little while contemplating them out of the corner of his eye; then suddenly he lifted his leg, urinated over the plans, and walked out without uttering a word.

There is a real difference between Napoleon's and Snowball's ideas. Napoleon argues that they need to increase food production; they'll starve to death if they waste time on the windmill. "Vote for Napoleon and the full manger" is his slogan.

NOTE: You may appreciate the dispute more if you know that just after the Civil War, a hard-hit, backward Soviet Union faced a choice—fast, all-out industrialization (Trotsky's plan) or more attention to agriculture. A better-known difference between Trotsky and Stalin was the emphasis on spreading the Revolution to other countries (Trotsky) or on building socialism in one country (Stalin). Orwell dismisses this in one paragraph about the defense of the farm (by using pigeons to stir up rebellion on other farms or by arming themselves) and concentrates on the windmill; it's more fun to read about than pigeons.

In the middle of the decisive Meeting, when Snowball has shouted down the sheep and made "a passionate appeal in favor of the windmill," showing them how the mill's electricity would "operate threshing machines, ploughs, harrows, rollers, reapers, binders, besides supplying every stall with its own electric light, hot and cold water, and an electric heater," Napoleon stands up and, "casting a peculiar side-long look at Snowball" (the precise detail that helps fix the scene in our minds) gives out a strange "high-pitched whimper." Nine huge dogs come bounding in and charge at Snowball. He just manages to escape with his life and get off the Farm.

Remember Napoleon's interest in the education of the nine puppies? His ferocious guard dogs are the result. Now, surrounded by his dogs, he announces to the "silent and terrified" animals that there will be no more Meetings. All farm questions will be settled at private meetings by a special committee of pigs, presided over by himself—no more time-wasting debates. Once again, as at public Meetings in the past, the animals—who are "dismayed"—just can't find the words to express themselves.

> Even Boxer was vaguely troubled. He set his ears back, shook his forelock several times, and tried hard to marshall his thoughts; but in the end he could not think of anything to say.

Language seems to belong to the elite. Some of the other pigs try to protest. But for those four young porkers, the new dictator has a crushing argument: "the dogs sitting around Napoleon let out deep, menacing growls, and the pigs fell silent." Police terror works. And so does Party discipline and conformity: "the sheep broke out into a tremendous bleating of 'Four legs good, two legs bad!' which went on for nearly a quarter of an hour and put an end to any chance of discussion."

It is not only power that is consolidated in this chapter, it is also a certain kind of language: the political Lie. The lie is prepared for by Squealer's speech explaining Napoleon's takeover, which is very similar to his hypocritical milk-and-apples speech in Chapter III, only much longer. First, the usual bit about Napoleon's "sacrifice" in taking on this extra work, then a popular antidemocratic argument that we all need the Leader to protect us against ourselves, against wrong decisions . . .

> Suppose you had decided to follow Snowball, with his moonshine of windmills—Snowball, who, as we now know, was no better than a criminal?

No one has ever mentioned—much less proved— that Snowball is a criminal. How then could the animals "know" it? By the fact of his punishment, of course.

Still, "somebody" does object that he fought bravely at the Battle of the Cowshed. This leads to an insinuation that prepares the Lie, the rewriting of history: "as to the Battle of the Cowshed," says Squealer, "the time will come when we shall find that Snowball's part in it was much exaggerated." The "watchword," Squealer concludes, is "iron discipline"—and the clincher, once again, is the threat that Jones may come back.

To swallow all this, the animals need faith. That is what Boxer—and apparently the others too—have, since he "voiced the general feeling by saying" what will be his second maxim: in addition to his private motto "I will work harder," he now has "Napoleon is always right."

At the Sunday ceremony that has replaced Meetings, the animals are now required to march past the skull of Major in a reverent way. As the substance of Major's teachings vanishes, he becomes revered as a saint in the new religion of Animalism.

The main function of these assemblies, however, is for the animals to receive their orders for the week. And soon "the animals were somewhat surprised to hear Napoleon announce that the windmill was to be built after all." No reasons are given, even though great sacrifices will be demanded to build it. How can even Squealer find the words to justify this great switch?

> Napoleon had never in reality been opposed to the windmill. On the contrary, it was he who had advocated it in the beginning, and the plan which Snowball had drawn on the floor . . . had actually been stolen from among Napoleon's papers. The windmill was, in fact, Napoleon's own creation.

Then why had he attacked the idea? "He had seemed to oppose the windmill, simply as a manoeuvre to get rid of Snowball, who was a dangerous character". . . "This," said Squealer, "was something called tactics." He repeated a number of times, "Tactics, comrades, tactics!"

NOTE: The Lie is swallowed partly because of the animals' need to believe in their leaders and partly because Squealer is a good propagandist, but mainly because force, or terror—in the form of the dogs—is on Napoleon's side. Orwell was, more than any other, the writer who saw the link in modern dictatorships between lying and terror.

CHAPTER VI

Like Chapter III, this chapter begins with hard but happy work. Here, however, the work is mostly for the windmill rather than for food. Something else is new, too: the pigs introduce a new policy of trade with their human neighbors. In fact, the pigs already seem to be becoming more like the old human masters themselves: they move into the farmhouse and sleep in beds. The animals take another look at the Seven Commandments and make a "discovery": the Fourth Commandment "really" reads "No animal shall sleep in a bed *with sheets*." The reader discovers, of course, that the pigs have for the first time changed a written commandment.

Finally, the nearly finished windmill collapses during a violent storm. Napoleon "knows" the saboteur: Snowball! We know that the Lie has taken on a new form: the government now has a scapegoat to blame for its failures.

"All that year the animals worked like slaves. But they were happy in their work; they grudged no effort or sacrifice"—The first sentences of this chapter, like the opening of Chapter III, contain in germ the whole point. The first part of the chapter is parallel to Chapter III, and contrasts ironically with it. The animals' subjection to the pigs has become increasingly evident—to us, but apparently not to them. The narrator relates the process with no comment; things seem to happen naturally, one after the other, as we have seen. This is one of Orwell's basic ironic techniques in *Animal Farm*: We know things the characters don't.

Thus the simple comparison "worked like slaves," which could simply mean that they worked very hard, is here charged with meaningful irony: the animals may not know it, but they really are becoming "slaves." Their sacrifice is not "for the benefit of themselves," as they think, but, we soon realize, for their new masters, the pigs.

Again the Lie, the perversion of language, is part of the process of enslavement. The animals work a 60-hour week, and Napoleon announces there'll be work on Sunday afternoons too—"strictly voluntary," but if the animals refuse, they'll have their rations cut in half. Apparently the word voluntary has been redefined. (In Orwell's next book, *1984*, government slogans like "WAR IS PEACE," and "FREEDOM IS SLAVERY," are similar redefinitions—the last one strikingly so.)

Still, most of the terribly hard work on the windmill does seem to be voluntary. The windmill is Orwell's image for Stalin's attempt to push all-out industrialization and mechanization on factory and farm, and animals seem to believe in it. Boxer, above all—who works harder than anyone else—has two slogans, we remember, which "seemed to him a sufficient answer to all problems": "I will work harder" and "Napoleon is always right." In the animals' belief and enthusiasm lie the sad irony of the first part of this chapter.

A further step is taken when Napoleon announces his "new policy" of trade with the humans. (The allegory is precise: this is the New Economic Policy inaugurated in 1921 by Lenin and ended in 1928. In *Animal Farm*, it doesn't end, it intensifies.) This produces "a vague uneasiness" in the animals. They remember—"or at least they thought they remembered"—passing resolutions against dealing with humans, money, trade.

NOTE: Technically, they are wrong; no resolutions were ever passed on this subject. You could argue, though, that Napoleon's new policy certainly violates the spirit of Commandments 1 and 2—and it certainly violates the policies advocated by Major in his speech.

Four young pigs try to speak against Napoleon's policy, but the growling dogs shut them up fast, and the sheep's repeated "Four legs good, two legs bad!" does the rest. Terror and drilled conformity are effective weapons.

The attempt is made to persuade, however: "Afterwards Squealer made a round of the farm and set the animals' minds at rest." Notice that Squealer is always explaining things privately, after the fact: no public discussion is allowed. First comes force, then comes propaganda. The idea of not trading with the humans, he says, is probably based on "lies circulated by Snowball." Thus, he continues to build on the lie begun in the last chapter and accelerated at the end of this one. When Squealer suggests they might even have dreamed the idea, because no such resolution exists in writing, they have to agree. Orwell was English, and in the British Isles, most of "the Constitution" is not written either; it is a collection of customs and legal precedents. You can see why this incident would be especially scary to an Englishman.

Once things are set in motion, they keep rolling. As, on their side, human beings begin to have a grudging respect for the animal-managed farm (although they still hate it), and as dealings with the humans pass unopposed on the animal side, the pigs themselves begin to take on a human lifestyle. They move into the farmhouse, where they sleep in beds. Notice how this is connected to the increasing personal power, privilege, and status of Napoleon. Not only do the pigs absolutely need "a quiet place to work in," but the farmhouse is

> more suited to the dignity of the Leader (for of late [Squealer] had taken to speaking of Napoleon under the title of 'Leader') to live in a house than in a mere sty.

That's the point, of course. The pigs—especially one pig—are increasingly in the same basic situation as the expelled human masters; why then shouldn't they have all the trappings? But justifying this means changing the past again.

Although Boxer simply repeats his "Napoleon is always right!" Clover has Muriel the goat, a good reader, check out the relevant Commandment for her. She finally makes out "No animal shall sleep in a bed *with sheets*," and we realize that for the first time the pigs have altered the written "unalterable law." Orwell tells us with his usual irony that "Curiously enough, Clover had not remembered that the Fourth Commandment mentioned sheets." And Squealer comes in with his usual speech about how the pigs have special needs. Then he ends with his customary Do-You-Want-Jones-to-Come-Back question. (The animals quickly "reassured him on this point.") The narrator informs us that this "put the whole matter in its proper perspective." Orwell's irony passes into sarcasm where Squealer is concerned.

The end of the chapter seems to resemble the beginning. With the coming of autumn, the animals are "tired but happy." They don't have much to eat, but the windmill makes their sacrifices seem well worth it. "Only old Benjamin refused to grow enthusiastic about the windmill . . . he would utter nothing beyond the cryptic remark that donkeys live a long time." Cryptic wisdom, as we'll see.

Then one night the half-finished windmill comes crashing down in the middle of a storm. At the site of the ruins, Napoleon

> paced to and fro in silence, occasionally snuffing at the ground. His tail had grown rigid and twitched sharply from side to side, a sign in him of intense mental activity.

Orwell doesn't want us to forget that the characters are animals—especially at key moments—as the description shows. This is a key moment, for Napoleon makes his longest speech of the book, a speech that sets in motion the terrible events of the next chapter:

> "Comrades," he said quietly, "do you know who is responsible for this? Do you know the enemy who has come in the night and overthrown our windmill? SNOWBALL! . . . Snowball has done this thing! In sheer malignity, thinking to set back our plans and avenge himself for his ignominious expulsion, this traitor has crept here under cover of night and destroyed our work of nearly a year. Comrades, I pronounce the death sentence upon Snowball . . ."

The speech is an illustration of the function of the scapegoat. If Snowball can be blamed for any failure, no matter the cause, then a. the Ruler remains infallible, whatever happens, and b. the emotions of the ruled can be played on at will. Napoleon announces that the windmill must be rebuilt at any cost, but it's going to be tough. He's going to need his scapegoat again.

CHAPTER VII

Things go from bad to worse in this chapter. It starts with hard times (hard work, cold winter, scarce food) and hard measures taken to deal with them (ruthless suppression of the revolt of the hens). When spring comes, there is growing hysteria about Snowball, whose invisible actions, like a witch's spells, are said to be responsible for all the farm's problems. In fact Squealer "demonstrates" that Snowball had been a traitor from the start. All this comes to a head when, in a special assembly, the dogs drag animal after animal out to Napoleon's feet, where they confess to all sorts of crimes they supposedly committed with Snowball, and the dogs immediately tear their throats out. The sickened, terrified animals seek consolation in singing "Beasts of England." Then Squealer announces that the song has just been forbidden, since it's a song of revolt for a better society, and that society has now been achieved.

NOTE: In this chapter the "charm" of the fable seems to have disappeared. Orwell is not trying to charm us, but to make us see terrible things. The killings seem real; so does the sorrow, and, more moving still, the bewilderment of the speechless animals.

Orwell was dealing with historical events that disturbed him deeply. From 1934 to 1939, the secret police arrested and interrogated, and deported or killed hundreds of thousands of people in the Soviet Union, mostly Communist Party officials, army officers, and their families and friends. Two series of public trials were held in Moscow, in which old Bolsheviks, who had made the Revolution and fought in the Civil War, confessed one after another to the most awful crimes. Most of them were condemned to death and shot.

What revolted Orwell was not only seeing the triumph of the Lie in the Moscow Trials themselves, but the spectacle closer to home of intellectuals in the British Left (of which he was a part, after all) either swallowing this nonsense or defending it as necessary.

As usual, Orwell sketches in the background with bare, swift strokes: "It was a bitter winter," he begins this chapter. With the hard weather and work somehow comes greater faith in the Leader's lies:

> Out of spite, the human beings pretended not to believe that it was Snowball who had destroyed the windmill: they said that it had fallen down because the walls were too thin. The animals knew that this was not the case.

But their actions ironically contradict what they "knew":

> Still, it had been decided to build the walls three feet thick this time instead of eighteen inches as before...

If there are lies to the animals about their problems, there are also lies to the humans. Mr. Whymper, the human agent through whom all their business is transacted, is shown sand-filled bins with grain on top, so that he will report to the outside world that there is no food shortage at Animal Farm.

But there is a real shortage of grain. Napoleon—who now is increasingly distant, surrounded only by growling dogs—sees no way out but to take the hens' eggs and sell them; the money will buy grain. Now, for the first time, there is "something resembling a rebellion." The hens want to keep their eggs, and rather than give them up, they lay their eggs from the rafters, smashing them on the floor. Napoleon acts "swiftly and ruthlessly." He simply cuts off their food. Five days later, they give in. Nine hens are dead. (Then more lies: it's reported they'd died of disease.)

NOTE: When Stalin decided that Russia needed large, mechanized, collective farms, and the *kulaks* (well-off peasants) refused to give up their private holdings, millions of them were deported or killed beginning in 1928 to 1929. Many of them felt so desperate that they slaughtered their own livestock.

Against this background of suffering, lying, and repression, the use of Snowball as a scapegoat grows and grows. First Snowball is reported to be in league with either Pilkington or Frederick, depending on which man Napoleon is thinking of dealing with at the moment. Then Snowball is reported to be performing all kinds of mischief on the farm, mostly under cover of darkness. Later we learn that the cows "declared unanimously that Snowball crept into their stalls and milked them in their sleep," and that Snowball is said to be in league with the rats.

All this leads directly to the rewriting of history. Snowball had to be a traitor from the start, everyone decides. The last stand for rationality, objective truth, and unalterable History is taken by the unintellectual Boxer, interestingly enough:

> He lay down, tucked his fore hoofs beneath him, shut his eyes, and with a hard effort managed to formulate his thoughts.
> "I do not believe that," he said. "Snowball fought bravely at the Battle of the Cowshed. I saw him myself."

Even when Squealer shows them that "secret documents" (which, unfortunately, Boxer can't read) "prove" Snowball's treason, Boxer, unlike the others, stands firm—until Squealer, "speaking very slowly and firmly," tells him that Napoleon "has stated categorically—categorically, comrade—that Snowball was Jones's agent from the very beginning." Then Faith—or conditioning—triumphs, and Boxer falls back on his slogan: "If Comrade Napoleon says it, it must be right." Squealer gives Boxer an "ugly look" and then warns the animals about "Snowball's secret agents lurking among us." The scene comes to a menacing close.

NOTE: We've seen that Orwell was intensely concerned with lying and hysteria in the Soviet Union, but perhaps he hits on a more general theme here. Is Squealer the only government official to use "secret documents" (which, unfortunately, the animals cannot see) to prove that things are as he said they are?

And what does Orwell imply about the way common people respond to outrageous government propaganda? Notice how hard Boxer tries to resist. It is, finally, his simple faith in the honesty and knowledge of his Leader that does him in—literally, as we'll see later. We've seen the implications of this kind of trust for totalitarian societies. Are there people in nontotalitarian countries who tend to believe that their Leader is always right?

The menace of the preceding scene is confirmed when Napoleon, surrounded by his huge growling dogs, summons the animals to assembly: "They all cowered silently in their places, seeming to know in advance that some terrible thing was about to happen." At a signal from Napoleon, the dogs seize four pigs by the ear and drag them, "squealing with pain and terror, to Napoleon's feet." Orwell has set the tone.

> The pigs' ears were bleeding, the dogs had tasted blood, and for a few moments they appeared to go quite mad. To the amazement of everybody, three of them flung themselves upon Boxer.

The "mad" violence is of course coldly and politically calculated. We know why Boxer is being attacked (remember that "ugly look" Squealer gave him?). When he pins a dog under his powerful hoof but then just looks to Napoleon for orders, we know he has lost his chance to stop the violence.

The four pigs, the same ones who protested when Napoleon abolished Meetings, confess to all kinds of crazy crimes. We may smile when they declare that "Snowball had privately admitted that he had been Jones's secret agent for years." But the swift, hard, "animal" detail that follows is very real and not funny at all: "When they finished their confession, the dogs promptly tore their throats out." Three hens, ringleaders in the egg rebellion, confess that "Snowball had appeared to them in a dream and incited them to disobey Napoleon's orders"; then other animals confess to hard-to-believe crimes, and all are killed.

> When it was all over, the remaining animals, except for the pigs and dogs, crept away in a body. They were shaken and miserable. They did not know which was more shocking—the treachery of the animals who had leagued themselves with Snowball, or the cruel retribution they had just witnessed.

Despite their solidarity, which is a solidarity of victims ("crept away in a body"), the animals still don't doubt what they are told. But their instinctive decency is revolted by these judicial murders. Above all, even if there had been slaughter under Jones, "it seemed to all of them far worse now that it was happening among themselves." A chilling thought. All together, "they all lie down" as though huddling together for warmth. Boxer is the only one who can find it in him to say a word: he resolves to "work harder" (his other

slogan) and goes off to do so. Clearly he is working off
his own confused and despairing feelings.

This dim feeling that the Revolution—the faith that
sustains them—has not been worth it after all swells
into a veritable lament in one of the most striking passages in the book. It centers around Clover, as the
animals are "huddled about [her], not speaking."
Through the animals' eyes we see the farm as it lies
before them on a spring evening.

> Never had the farm—and with a kind of surprise
> they remembered it was their own farm, every
> inch of it their own property—appeared to the ani-
> mals so desirable a place. As Clover looked down
> the hillside her eyes filled with tears.

The disillusion and sorrow are expressed wordlessly, as an immediate reaction, without analysis: the
farm doesn't really belong to them, we realize, no
more than it did when Jones was there. Ownership
means power, and the animals are powerless.

And now comes the only part of the book in which
Orwell enters the mind of one of his characters. It is all
the more moving for being the thoughts of Clover,
someone who cannot articulate them: "If she could
have spoken her thoughts, it would have been to
say . . ." Like millions of simple, decent, working people, Orwell is saying, Clover feels what is wrong:

> These scenes of terror and slaughter were not
> what they had looked forward to on that night
> when old Major first stirred them to rebellion.

And she longs for what is right, not for a theory, but
for an image:

> If she herself had had any picture of the future, it
> had been of a society of animals set free from hun-
> ger and the whip, all equal, each working accord-
> ing to his capacity, the strong protecting the weak,

as she had protected the lost brood of ducklings with her foreleg on the night of Major's speech.

Then she expresses a clear picture of just how far they have slipped from the ideal:

> Instead, they had come to a time when no one dared speak his mind, when fierce, growling dogs roamed everywhere, and when you had to watch your comrades torn to pieces after confessing to shocking crimes.

NOTE: There is a brutal irony in comparing the state of *Animal Farm* under Napoleon with the main points of Major's speech. It is an irony that Clover senses but does not precisely see. When Major talked of Man's exploitation and cruelty, he addressed the hens (he says their eggs were being taken from them), the young pigs (he says their throats would be cut within the year), and Boxer (he says he would be sold to the horse-slaughterer). Now after the Rebellion, when Man has been eliminated, the hens have faced the same fate they had under Man, and so have at least four of the young pigs. We'll see what happens to Boxer in Chapter IX.

Orwell suggests, without saying, how strong is Clover's habit of submission, her patience, her faith. He says that she'll continue to work, to obey Napoleon, to believe that things are better now than in the days of Jones. "But still"—and Orwell ends the passage with rhetorical repetition, closing with a moving, paradoxical reminder of how inarticulate she is—

> it was not for this that she and all the other animals had hoped and toiled. It was not for this that they had built the windmill and faced the bullets of Jones's guns. Such were her thoughts, though she lacked the words to express them.

It is precisely because she can't find words to express her thoughts that she begins to sing the song of the Rebellion, "Beasts of England." The others join in, and they sing it slowly and sadly, as they never have before.

And that's when Squealer tells them the song has just been forbidden, since the Rebellion is now "completed" and there's no need for it anymore. Orwell's irony has never been heavier.

The new song, written by Minimus—"Animal Farm, Animal Farm, Never through me shalt thou come to harm"—is, we note, a patriotic song rather than a revolutionary one.

CHAPTER VIII

Like the Battle of the Cowshed in Chapter IV, this is a light chapter wedged in between two heavy ones. If the Battle of the Windmill is much darker and more painful than the earlier battle, the fighting is still treated as a mock-epic. And the chapter ends with a couple of poker-faced jokes at the pigs' expense (although they're at the animals' expense, in a way).

There is a kind of prologue to this chapter—really an epilogue to the last one—which highlights the giant step the pigs have taken toward betraying the Revolution. It's a highlight we've seen before: a rewriting of an "unalterable law" follows a violation of that law by those in power. When Clover asks Muriel to read her the Sixth Commandment (Benjamin has already refused), she finds: "No animal shall kill any other animal *without cause.*" Once again the corruption of language—here, of a fundamental text—that accompanies the corruption of a political ideal. Power to change language, Orwell says, is power to change reality, and vice-versa.

As usual, Orwell treats the change with the irony of feigned ignorance. "Somehow or other," says the narrator, "the last two words had slipped out of the animals' memory."

Clearly, Napoleon is absolute dictator now. Orwell saw that modern dictators rely essentially on terror (as we saw in the last chapter), propaganda, and other ways of changing the present and the past through language. Now there is one final element in the psychology of totalitarian dictatorship. It is an extension of the faith in Snowball's diabolical wrongness and Napoleon's infallible rightness: absolute adoration of the dictator as a kind of god on earth.

NOTE: Napoleon's wildly shifting alliances—and the switch in the propaganda line that goes with them—are like the changes in Stalin's policy toward the West in the 1930s and early 40s. Distrusting the democratic nations as much as the fascists, Stalin first sent out the line that there was no difference between any of the non-Communists, fascist or otherwise; subsequently, as the Nazi menace grew, the fascists became the enemy of mankind; then, in August 1939, Stalin signed a nonagression pact and other agreements with Hitler, the German Nazi dictator. Finally, after Germany invaded Russia in 1941, everything changed again. What infuriated Orwell was the way Soviet sympathizers in the West managed to instantly develop a whole new set of beliefs with each change in the Soviet position.

It is not Napoleon's brilliance that wins the Battle of the Windmill, however; it is the collective rage of the animals that drives out the invader, at great sacrifice. And that sacrifice is terrible indeed, so that when the bleeding, wounded animals hear a gun firing for a victory celebration amidst the ruins of their "windmill," they don't even understand what it is. Yet Napoleon manages to use the war as an excuse to heap more glory upon himself:

> It was announced that the battle would be called the Battle of the Windmill and that Napoleon had created a new decoration, the Order of the Green Banner, which he had conferred upon himself.

Anyone who has ever had a hangover will appreciate Orwell's ironic joke on Napoleon and the other pigs. When Squealer appears the Morning After the victory party, "walking slowly and dejectedly, his eyes dull, his tail hanging limply behind him," and "looking seriously ill"—and especially when the rumor goes round that Napoleon is dying, and he solemnly decrees the death penalty for drinking—we don't need to be told what is happening. The ironic technique Orwell uses to make his joke is the same technique he has used to make his serious points about the loss of liberty and the alteration of the truth: we know more than the animals do.

At the end of the chapter, nobody (well, "hardly anyone") can understand why Squealer is found sprawled next to the ladder and the paintpot on the barn floor one night. When a few days later Muriel notices that there's yet another Commandment they've "remembered wrong"—"No animal shall drink alcohol *to excess*"—neither the narrator nor the animals make the connection.

CHAPTER IX

Most readers have found this the most moving and memorable chapter in the book. By inventing the episode of Boxer's death—which, unlike other episodes in this allegory, does not stand for any specific event in history—Orwell has found a way to dramatize everything that's wrong with the new society. Here we can feel the full impact of the pigs' callous betrayal of the working animals, their betrayal of the revolutionary ideal.

Fittingly, the first half of the chapter gives a general picture of how things now stand in the new society. The picture is painted with Orwell's usual irony. Watch for the themes of sacrifice ("Boxer's split hoof" at the very start is a tangible sign of this), hard times, the animals' belief in the revolutionary ideal and hope for the future. (The new concepts of "retirement" and "pension" are signs of this.) And notice, in ironic counterpoint throughout, the obvious signs—obvious to us but not to the animals—that this society is a dictatorship and an oligarchy (rule by one single group, in this case, the pigs).

The themes all come together at the beginning of the chapter. Boxer is consoled in his thought of the windmill to be rebuilt yet again and by his belief in his coming retirement to the barley-field. But if we've been reading carefully, we've seen that the field was set aside for barley in the last chapter, when the pigs bought books on brewing and distilling after the drinking-party. We already have an ironic hint of what's to come. (Beer, we remember, is made with barley.)

"Meanwhile life was hard." When it comes to hard times, Orwell is always as stark and simple as what he is describing. The winter is cold and food rations are reduced—except for the pigs and dogs—with this ironic justification: "A too rigid equality in rations, Squealer explained, would have been contrary to the principles of Animalism." The narrator doesn't comment on this blatant contradiction of everything the revolution was supposed to stand for, but we as readers can't miss it.

Then Squealer rattles off lists of figures proving that things were worse in the past, and are getting better all the time on Animal Farm. "The animals believed every word of it." For one thing, no one remembers clearly what it was like under Jones anymore. Once again, history is rewritten by the propaganda of those in power.

The farm prospers, but the animals do not. In fact their food rations must be cut again because money is needed for building materials. The signs of overwhelming inequality pile up, always presented without comment by the narrator, as if all this is quite natural. One afternoon there's an unknown "warm, rich, appetizing scent" in the air, the smell of barley cooking, perhaps. "The animals sniffed the air hungrily and wondered whether a warm mash was being prepared for their supper." They feel a simple, limited hope; Orwell brings the feeling home to us with concrete details that tell us worlds about the animal's condition:

> But no warm mash appeared, and on the following Sunday it was announced that from now onwards all barley would be reserved for the pigs. . . . every pig was now receiving a ration of a pint of beer daily, with half a gallon for Napoleon himself. . . .

Then the social side of life is described: ceremonies and celebrations, all presented ironically as adding "dignity" to life, comforting reminders that "they were truly their own masters." The Farm is proclaimed a Republic, and the animals have an election for President. "There was only one candidate, Napoleon, who was elected unanimously." At the same time, history is rewritten further: Snowball, the pigs now claim, was not only in league with Jones from the start, but actually led the human forces at the Battle of the Cowshed! As Snowball gains in evil (fantastically), Napoleon gains in good (fantastically).

Moses the raven comes back with his tales of Sugarcandy Mountain. The pigs say these are lies (although they let him stay on the farm without working, with a mug of beer a day, interestingly enough) but many animals believe him: "Their lives now, they reasoned, were hungry and laborous; was it not right and just that a better world should exist somewhere else?"

This is the background for the story of the last days of Boxer.

Orwell sets the story up by making Boxer's collapse a dramatic event for the community, reminding us that it was his strength and sacrifices that saved the Farm again and again: there is a "rumor," then the "news" that Boxer has collapsed, then half the animals on the farm come running. His loss of all strength is described in precise detail:

> There lay Boxer, between the shafts of the cart, his neck stretched out, unable even to raise his head. His eyes were glazed, his sides matted with sweat. A thin stream of blood had trickled out of his mouth.

His thoughts for the next two days will be about his retirement to a corner of the pasture where he hopes to spend his last years peacefully improving his mind ("learning the remaining twenty-two letters of the alphabet"), if possible in the company of Benjamin. Squealer, full of sympathy, announces that Comrade Napoleon's concern for "one of the most loyal workers on the farm" has led him to arrange to have Boxer treated by a veterinary surgeon in the town hospital.

The next day, while the animals are weeding tur-
nips ("under the supervision of a pig," Orwell tells us
in passing), Benjamin comes galloping toward them.
It's the first time anyone has ever seen Benjamin gallop. "They're taking Boxer away!" he shouts. "Without waiting for orders from the pig" (says the narrator
in passing, once again reminding us of the inequality
that reigns here) the animals race to the farm buildings. They see a van and Boxer's stall is empty. They
crowd around, shouting good-bye to Boxer. "Fools!
Fools!" Benjamin shouts. "Do you not see what is
written on the side of the van?" There is a hush. For
the only time in the book, Benjamin, who knows how
to read well but has decided that nothing is worth
reading, does read something—the sign on the
truck—out loud. It is the sign of a horse slaughterer.
They all cry out in horror to Boxer to save himself, as
the van drives off and they see his face at the small
window at the back. And now Orwell gives us an
image that fixes the scene in our minds, a sound that
may stay with you long after you've finished the
book:

> a moment later his face disappeared from the win-
> dow and there was the sound of a tremendous
> drumming of hoofs inside the van. He was trying
> to kick his way out.

Before he exhausted his strength working overtime
for Animal Farm, "a few kicks from Boxer's hoofs
would have smashed the van to matchwood." But not
anymore: "in a few moments the sound of drumming
hoofs grew fainter and died away."

That's the last they ever see of Boxer. When
Squealer comes in with a tearful picture of Boxer's last
moments in the hospital, having received "every

attention a horse could have," his hypocrisy is particularly painful. So is his attempt to explain the "foolish and wicked rumor" that Boxer was sent to the knacker's (the horse slaughterer): "surely they knew their beloved Leader, Comrade Napoleon, better than that?" The van had been the property of the knacker, and the vet who bought it didn't have time to paint out the old sign. "The animals were enormously relieved to hear this," says the narrator. No comment.

When the pigs hold a memorial banquet in Boxer's honor, a grocer delivers a large wooden crate to the farmhouse, and the sounds of uproarious singing and finally of a quarrel and broken glass are heard late in the night. When the pigs get up late the next day, the word goes out that "from somewhere or other pigs had acquired the money to buy themselves another case of whiskey." End of chapter.

NOTE: The description of Boxer's fate is full of irony. Once again the narrator pretends not to know something that we know because of him—but the animals don't know. The irony is at its bitterest here. And there is another irony in the story itself. Boxer's last sacrifice has been to be slaughtered in order to procure drinking money for the pigs. Major's prophetic incitement to Revolution—"You, Boxer, the very day that those great muscles of yours lose their power, Jones will sell you to the knacker, who will cut your throat"—has been fulfilled, ironically, not by the human Jones but by the animals who have taken over the Revolution. The question dimly sensed by Clover earlier is implicitly posed again, with pressing force: if this is what you get, why revolt? What was the Revolution for?

This is a basic question. We can ask it about the Russian Revolution—and Orwell's answer about that will be made quite clear in the next chapter, in case we still had any doubts. But we can also ask it about revolution in general, or even about any attempt to make a more just society. You'll want to think about this question again when you've finished the book.

CHAPTER X

Just about everything that has been implied in *Animal Farm* so far is made explicit in this last chapter.

Like Chapter IX, it begins with a general portrait of the "new" society. The same themes are there, sad or ironic, made all the more poignant by the passage of time. Memory of the old days is fading; history as we know it has disappeared. Times are hard, but it is said they were harder still under Jones. Above all, the animals still have their revolutionary faith: the farm is theirs, they believe—the world will one day be theirs—they work for themselves—all animals are equal.

In a series of dramatic demonstrations, their faith is utterly stripped away from them. Orwell pushes his allegorical narrative from past history (the Russian Revolution) to future prophecy: the pigs will openly reveal themselves to be absolutely identical to men.

After the high drama of Boxer's death and the bitter irony of its aftermath, Orwell seems to be winding things down. The opening portrait of the Farm is sketched simply, as usual, but with a philosophical distance and tone:

> Years passed. The seasons came and went, the short animal lives fled by.

Clover is old and stout, two years past the age to retire, "but in fact no animal had ever actually retired," says the narrator matter-of-factly. The farm has prospered and all kinds of machinery are in use, which helps to bring in money (but not increased comforts or leisure for the animals). And then we have an explicit statement of something that was suggested before, but never actually said: "Somehow it seemed as though the farm had grown richer without making the animals themselves any richer—except, of course, for the pigs and the dogs."

It's almost as if the animals themselves are becoming more aware. But in the rest of the passage, this consciousness is removed and the narrator's poker-faced irony increases. We are told that there are many pigs, many dogs (the bureaucracy and the police have multiplied); they do work, but it's work that the "other animals were too ignorant to understand":

> the pigs had to expend enormous labors every day upon mysterious things called "files," "reports," "minutes," and "memoranda." These were large sheets of paper which had to be closely covered with writing, and as soon as they were so covered, they were burnt in the furnace.

When Orwell reduces managerial office-work to a pure physical description ("sheets of paper closely covered with writing") he reduces it to absurdity. It's an effective satiric technique.

The ironic satire takes on a special bite when we are

told that "still, neither pigs nor dogs produced any food by their own labor." This is just about what Major said of Man (and what Marx said of the bourgeoisie) at the very beginning of the book. Have we come full circle?

Apparently we have, because the next paragraph tells us that "for the others, their life, so far as they knew, was as it had always been." And after giving a stark picture of basic animal life (hungry, sleeping on straw, laboring outside, cold in winter, bothered by flies in summer), Orwell returns to the function of history: since the animals can no longer remember life before the Rebellion, they can't be sure if things are better or worse, whether the Revolution was worth it or not. They have no standard of comparison. All they have to go on is Squealer's figures, "which invariably demonstrated that everything was getting better and better." Only old Benjamin is sure that things are never better or worse, "hunger, hardship, and disappointment being, so he said, the unalterable law of life." (Does *Animal Farm* bear him out?)

But there is one difference. The animals believe in the Revolution. "They were still the only farm in the whole county—in all England!—owned and operated by animals." They are proud of their flag. They have no two-legged masters. They are all equal.

One day Squealer takes the sheep out to a private piece of land to teach them something new. At this point Orwell shifts from an allegory of the past and present into a vision of the future.

We are prepared for something dramatic, just after the sheep return, by "the terrified neighing of a horse," then the startled animals watching, until finally they see—with one sentence making an entire paragraph, to increase the effect—a pig walking on his hind legs. Then out come all the pigs, walking. Napoleon is the last:

> there was a tremendous baying of dogs and a shrill crowing from the black cockerel, and out came Napoleon himself, majestically upright, casting haughty glances from side to side, and with his dogs gambolling round him.
> He carried a whip in his trotter.

After the shock caused by this vision wears off a little, the animals, despite their years of never complaining, never criticizing, are just about to say something, perhaps, when . . .

> all the sheep burst out into a tremendous bleating of—"Four legs good, two legs *better!* Four legs good, two legs *better!* Four legs good, two legs *better!*"

This is the final transformation of Major's dream. It has gone from vision to doctrine to slogan; now it is the absolute opposite of what he had said. The form of the dream remains (the slogan, something the animals have invented), but the content is just as it was under their human masters. What about the Commandments themselves?

Clover and Benjamin provide the answer:

> Benjamin felt a nose nuzzling his shoulder. He looked round. It was Clover. Her old eyes looked dimmer than ever. Without saying anything, she tugged gently at his mane and led him round to the end of the big barn, where the Seven Commandments were written.

And when she asks him to read what is on the wall, Benjamin for once agrees. There is only one Commandment left:

ALL ANIMALS ARE EQUAL
BUT SOME ANIMALS ARE MORE EQUAL
THAN OTHERS

The process of rewriting history has been completed. The new slogan says it all.

In a sense this is the climax of the book, but Orwell has also imagined a kind of epilogue to dramatize what the animals have just read. He leads into it by an "After that . . ." After that, it does not seem strange when the pigs take on all the habits of humans, down to the last detail. And we have some comic examples—such as the subscriptions the pigs take out to *John Bull*, *Tit-Bits*, and the *Daily Mirror*.

The last episode in the book describes a visit of humans to the farm. Orwell gives us a strong image in passing to suggest, visually, the meaning of this visit, the condition of the animals, and what the Rebellion has become. When the neighboring farmers arrive,

> The animals were weeding the turnip field. They worked diligently, hardly raising their faces from the ground, and not knowing whether to be more frightened of the pigs or of the human visitors.

Pigs and humans are already united in their "superiority" to the animals—in the fear they inspire.

But Orwell will go further. He'll use the device of the drinking party once again. But this time pigs and humans are all together. And they are directly, not indirectly, observed by the curious animals (all together again), who creep into the farmhouse garden and watch fearfully through the windows. This is a symbolic image. Those who work are not admitted to the feast.

Beer is going round, and Pilkington is making a speech. His main point is his feeling of friendship for Animal Farm now that he sees there's nothing threatening in it for humans. They'd been nervous in the past about the effects of the Rebellion on their own animals, "or even upon their human employees," but now he realizes there's nothing to worry about: "discipline and orderliness" reign. What he means by this is clear enough:

> He believed that he was right in saying that the lower animals on Animal Farm did more work and received less food than any animals in the country.

The irony works neatly. Pilkington's praise is more damning than any condemnation could be. He concludes with a witticism (he thinks it's witty, and so do the pigs) that drives the point home:

> "If you have your lower animals to contend with,
> . . . we have our lower classes!"

Napoleon replies with a speech pledging friendship in return. To cement "normal business relations" with their neighbors, in fact, he is going to eliminate the last vestiges of the Rebellion: the flag, the terms of address (no more "Comrade"), the ceremonies, and even the name of the farm will be changed: "Henceforward the farm was to be known as 'The Manor Farm.' "

We may think that Orwell can go no further in driving home his point: there is no difference whatsoever between this farm and the others.

But he does go further. The animals creep away after this, but they rush back a few moments later when there is the sound of quarreling. As they watch the pigs quarreling with the men (it seems Pilkington and Napoleon had both played the ace of spades), they realize that all the fat faces in the room—pig or man—are the same: "it was impossible to say which was which."

NOTE: What is the moral of this pessimistic fable? Some readers have viewed *Animal Farm* as a perfect illustration of the famous saying associated with the British historian, Lord Acton: "All power corrupts, but absolute power corrupts absolutely." The more power the pigs gain, the more corrupt they become. One by one, they take on all the human vices: smoking, drinking, etc. Napoleon, who has absolute power, is the one who drinks most. But is the moral corruption of the pigs the main focus of *Animal Farm?* Or is it their increasing resemblance to humans, to political masters?

You may see another, purely political moral in the work: that the Russian Revolution wasn't worth it, or, more generally, that revolution just isn't worth it. But whatever happens in the story, *no one* "wants Jones back." (Do you?) You may find it interesting to think about this pessimistic—but not utterly pessimistic—pronouncement of Orwell's: "All revolutions are failures, but they are not the same failure." Some revolutions may be more "worth it" than others.

Similarly, Orwell thought that any mature person knew that life has more unhappiness than happiness in it: the problem is, once you realize that, how should you live? By what values? Orwell chose to fight for truth and decency as he saw them.

Or you may conclude that the moral of *Animal Farm* is broadly philosophical rather than political, that Benjamin, for example, sums it up in the last chapter: "hunger, hardship and disappointment" are "the unalterable law of life." But what then? Surely Orwell, for one, felt it was worth struggling to change that "unalterable law." Despite everything.

Animal Farm is a fable about rulers and ruled, oppressors and oppressed, and an ideal betrayed. The particular meaning we give it will depend partly on our own political beliefs—"political" in the deepest sense of the word. The book is there to be enjoyed, to enrich—and perhaps change—our thinking and feeling about how human beings can best live together in this world.

A STEP BEYOND

Tests and Answers

TESTS

Test 1

1. In *Animal Farm* George Orwell makes the   _____
point that
   A. to the victor belongs the spoils
   B. power corrupts, and absolute power
      corrupts absolutely
   C. Communism is the most evil form of
      government

2. *Animal Farm* illustrates   _____
   A. the deterioration into tyranny of a
      political system that began full of
      promise
   B. the wisdom of not forming alliances
   C. the basic animalistic nature of humanity

3. The novel is   _____
   A. devoid of humor
   B. a mixture of humor and seriousness
   C. best understood as a comedy in which
      animals assume human traits

4. The Battle of the Windmill represents   _____
   A. the Animals' attempt to mechanize the
      Farm

B. the Russian Civil War
C. Germany's invasion of the Soviet Union in World War II

5. Which are correctly paired? ———
   A. Farmer Jones—the Czar of Russia
   B. Major—Stalin
   C. Napoleon—Hitler

6. In the final scene the pigs are indistinguishable from ———
   A. each other
   B. the humans
   C. the other animals

7. Napoleon made the mistake of ———
   A. accepting counterfeit notes
   B. trusting Squealer
   C. siding with Frederick against Pilkington

8. The animals who confess their crimes are ———
   A. pardoned
   B. jailed
   C. executed

9. Napoleon says he is abolishing the singing of "Beasts of England" because ———
   A. the song had limited appeal to the newer generation
   B. the hope expressed in the song had already been realized
   C. it distracted the animals from their work

10. In the end, the sheep are bleating ———
    A. "Four legs good, two legs bad"
    B. "Four legs good, two legs better"
    C. "Animals are equal to humans"

11. Why does Orwell use animals for characters?

12. Compare *Animal Farm* and *1984*.

13. There is an animated cartoon film of *Animal Farm* with a happy ending: animals on other farms realize Napoleon has set up a dictatorship; they rise up and overthrow him. Is this ending a good idea?

14. Is *Animal Farm* an attack on socialism?

15. Discuss the significance of *Animal Farm* as an allegory.

Test 2

1. Squealer   _____
   A. acts as the middleman when Napoleon has to deal with humans
   B. offers explanations for every move taken by the leadership
   C. is the only individualist on the farm

2. Which is *not* true of Benjamin the donkey?   _____
   A. He offers no opinion on the Revolution
   B. He says life will go on as always—badly
   C. He has no friends on the farm

3. Before Snowball was expelled, Napoleon gave the highest priority to   _____
   A. the education of the young
   B. building a windmill
   C. following the Seven Commandments of Animalism

4. Boxer's slogan was   _____
   A. "The fruits of our labors belong to us!"
   B. "The Revolution will succeed!"
   C. "I will work harder!"

5. Boxer is ultimately   _____
   A. retired and rewarded for his faithful service
   B. blamed for the loss of the windmill
   C. sold to the knacker

6. Almost caught red-handed in the act of changing the Commandments is   _____
   A. Muriel the goat
   B. the cat
   C. Squealer

7. The scapegoat for the shortcomings of Napoleon's regime is   _____
   A. Snowball

B. Boxer

C. the neighboring humans

8. The raven, with his promise of Sugarcandy _____
   Mountain for the animals after they die,
   A. is forever banished from Animal Farm
   B. sides first with Snowball, then with
      Napoleon
   C. is banished but is allowed to return and
      given daily rations though he does no
      work

9. The Seven Commandments are later _____
   reduced to one:
   A. All animals are equal
   B. Four legs good, two legs bad
   C. Contact with humans corrupts

10. Mollie, the white mare, _____
    A. saves Boxer in the Battle of the Cowshed
    B. has a weakness for ribbons and sugar
    C. learned the alphabet more easily than
       the other horses

11. Judging from *Animal Farm*, what does Orwell's own
    political philosophy seem to be?

12. The "Commandment" *All animals are equal, but some animals are more equal than others* has become famous. Why?
    What significance does this "Commandment" have in
    the context of the story?

13. Discuss the image of the Leader in *Animal Farm*.

14. Discuss the satiric techniques used in *Animal Farm*.

15. Does *Animal Farm* have a hero?

ANSWERS

Test 1

1. B   **2.** A   **3.** B   **4.** C   **5.** A   **6.** B

7. A   **8.** C   **9.** B   **10.** B

11.   Orwell's main concerns in this book are political (how people act together, how societies function) and satiric (to attack-with-a-smile). For both of these purposes, types rather than complex characters are most useful; individual psychology would just get in Orwell's way. Then, too, he wanted a story with humor and charm that he could tell simply, a story that could be widely translated; the animal fable is perfect for these reasons. You'll want to give some specific examples of Orwell's humorous and satiric use of combinations of human-and-animal traits.

12.   The last two books Orwell wrote have much in common. Their main concerns are political and their themes are similar. *1984* can be seen as the sequel to *Animal Farm: Animal Farm* concerns the rise of a totalitarian dictatorship; in *1984*, totalitarianism has utterly triumphed. "Newspeak" in *1984* is a logical development from the corruption of language we've noted in *Animal Farm*. The rewriting of history has developed tremendously in *1984*; that's Winston Smith's job! Cruelty is enormously developed in *1984*, as is, obviously, repression. As for inequality, the proles in *1984* bear a curious and disturbing resemblance to the animals in *Animal Farm*.

The basic and obvious difference is that *1984* is a novel with human characters. The humor and charm of the beast fable was the last thing Orwell wanted in *1984*. Still, Orwell's final novel can make us more aware of the grim warning implicit in *Animal Farm*.

13.   Definitely not! It misses the political point of *Animal Farm*: at the end of the book the old slaves are slaves again, despite their Rebellion, and will remain so indefinitely. That was the message Orwell intended to convey; he certainly didn't believe there was an easy answer to the problem. *Animal Farm* is a work of despair and very little hope.

A happy ending to *Animal Farm* would also make an artistic mess of the whole story: *Animal Farm* progresses logically, inexorably, toward the last scene (almost like tragedy), so much so that, like Clover, we have a hard time saying how we got there. To add an extra episode to Orwell's ending is to destroy his beautifully structured whole.

14. This is debatable. It certainly is an attack on Soviet Communism: Napoleon equals Stalin, the pigs equal Communist bureaucrats, etc. Inequality and oppression are brought about through the use of propaganda (Squealer) and terror (the dogs). Then, too, a basic belief of Major (Marx) is ferociously disproved in the book: just get rid of Man (capitalists), he told the animals, and everything will be great. They do and they end up as badly off as they were before revolting.

But Orwell himself said that everything he wrote after 1937 was "against totalitarianism and for democratic socialism," so clearly he would want to make a distinction. If it seems to you that Major's speech is presented as a worthwhile ideal, if the animals' happiness in the early days of the Revolution is not presented ironically as an illusion (Chapter II), then you will see evidence of Orwell's positive attitude toward socialism in *Animal Farm*. Remember, though, that some readers have seen those episodes as satires of socialist ideals. The most convincing argument that the book is not an attack on socialism is what happens to the pigs: they turn into *men*—in other words, they become the capitalist enemy they originally set out to overthrow. In Orwell's view that appears to have been the worst thing that could have happened to them. And take a good look at Pilkington, who represents the capitalist democracies of Britain and France: does Orwell make him a particularly attractive character?

Remember, too, that whatever your views about socialism may be, the question asks you about Orwell's. You might come to the conclusion that the fable satirizes both capitalism and socialism. That would make it a negative work indeed. Or you might want to return to Orwell's distinction between "socialism" and Soviet dictatorship.

15. This is a difficult question that you need to break down into sections. Try distinguishing different types of allegory such as 1. political allegory, in which the dogs represent the Secret Police, and 2. historical allegory, in which the Battle of the Cowshed parallels the Civil War. To be an allegory, of course, an episode does not have to refer to a specific historical event. The death of Boxer, for instance, has political significance, but is not a statement about the death of any particular individual.

Test 2

1. B   **2.** C   **3.** A   **4.** C   **5.** C   **6.** C

7. A   **8.** C   **9.** B   **10.** B

11. You may conclude that Orwell's philosophy in this book is purely negative: we know he detests Soviet Communism, and he doesn't seem to have any great affection for capitalism, either. Most of his sympathy is for the common people (the animals), which would put him in the camp of the Left (and of course this view is supported by the rest of his work). On the other hand, seeing the working class as "animals" doesn't exactly lead you to socialism.

Perhaps you can explain that Orwell does promote a set of definite political values, even if he doesn't outline a coherent political philosophy. These values include:

1. love of honesty (hatred of lying)
2. respect for common decency (Clover, Boxer)
3. love of freedom (hatred of repression and dictators)
4. desire for equality (hatred of inequality and oppression).

The last point is the most problematic: what if there is a natural hierarchy, what if some people *really are* more equal than others? This question is implied in *Animal Farm* in a way that perhaps Orwell himself did not see. But then, he was a man who struggled all his life with his own feelings about the social class system.

Finally, we may see in *Animal Farm* a lament for revolution rather than an attack on it. If only, Orwell seems to be saying, if only revolutionaries could be true to their own ideals!

12. This formula is a paradox, of course: nothing can be "more equal" than anything (or anybody) else. Thus it neatly expresses the hypocrisy of those who preach equality and neither practice it nor really believe in it. Apparently there are many people like that, for the expression has become proverbial.

In the context of *Animal Farm*, the "Commandment" is

1. the final, ironic redefinition of an important word.

2. the final Commandment to be rewritten, and thus the ultimate example of the pigs' control over language, "history," and "truth."

3. a double reverse twist. The expression tells the truth: the pigs are "more equal," that is, superior in status to all the other animals.

13. The only leader who is not treated with ferocious satire is Major, and he is a. an intellectual leader only, and b. quickly dead and out of the way. The arch-leader is Napoleon, and he doesn't lead, he takes all power unto himself. Once in battle he actually "leads" from behind (Chapter VIII), although he is no coward. He drinks, is flattered outrageously, and appears "in triumph" like a king or god. All of this is seen from the outside, as actions or functions in the mechanism of dictatorship: we don't know what Napoleon himself thinks or feels, and Orwell clearly doesn't care.

14. You'll want to break your answer down into categories. Here are some examples:

1. *Caricatures:* Mr. Jones (negligence and stupidity), Squealer (hypocrisy)
2. *Parodies:* Major's speech (in Chapter I)
                Napoleon's speeches
                Minimus' poem and anthem
3. *Irony:* The basic ironic technique of *Animal Farm* is that of feigned ignorance (see, for example, the pigs' drinking party). But this technique has a wide range of effects, from farce (the drinking party) to the deep, basic contradiction between the animals' beliefs—presented with no comment by the narrator—and the realities the reader is able to see or deduce.

Finally, the satire in *Animal Farm* is not always meant to be funny. Pick some satiric episodes that do seem funny to you and some that don't. The ones that aren't funny will probably concern the basic target of satire in *Animal Farm:* a system that maintains inequality and oppression in the name of freedom and equality.

15. Some readers have seen Boxer as the hero: he saves the Farm again and again, in war and in work; in fact, he gives his life for the Farm—a kind of tragic hero, he has the flaw of blind faith. He is "too good"; his decency (or is it his stupidity?) blinds him to the real motives of those whom he serves with his great strength.

On the other hand, you might argue that Boxer simply isn't around that much in the fable. Because we never know Boxer's thoughts—except for his two repeated maxims— and because he is not at all the driving force behind any of the action, it's rather hard to see him as the hero of the book. You might want to argue that *Animal Farm* has a collective hero: the animals. Or that, after all, why look for a hero at all? Orwell is concerned with politics in this book, not with individuals.

Term Paper Ideas

1. Write an allegorical animal fable of your own, using political events in the United States over the past few years for your "other story."

2. Compare *Animal Farm* with any other fable you know.

3. Discuss Benjamin's character and philosophy in the context of the story.

4. Discuss the friendship of Boxer and Benjamin.

5. How does each one of the animals, through action or neglect, contribute to the pigs' takeover?

6. Analyze the significance of the last scene in *Animal Farm*.

7. One critic said Major's speech was "obviously ridiculous." Do you agree?

8. Discuss the treatment of war in *Animal Farm*.

9. Orwell thought the idea of substituting another animal for the pigs was idiotic. Why?

10. Discuss the role of the human beings in *Animal Farm*.

11. Discuss the role of the sheep in the story.

12. In what senses is the society depicted in *Animal Farm* "totalitarian," by the end of the book?

13. Are there any differences, for the animals, between life at the end of the book and life under Jones?

14. Find the places in the story where Orwell mentions food. What is the function of food in the story?

15. Discuss the role of reading in *Animal Farm*: who reads, how well, how much, why, and when.

16. Why do you think Orwell subtitled his book "A Fairy Story"?

17. *Animal Farm* has sold well over 1 million copies in English, and has been translated into 14 languages. Why do you think it is so popular?

18. Why does the windmill keep reappearing in the story?

19. Why does the Rebellion break out?

20. Suppose you wanted to write a one-sentence moral for *Animal Farm* and put it in italics at the end of the story. What would that moral be, and why?

21. A critic who didn't like *Animal Farm* has said that the real source of the work is *The Tale of Pigling Bland* and other children's stories by Beatrix Potter; others have spoken of Swift's *Gulliver's Travels* as Orwell's inspiration. If you know either work—or better still, both—comment on these claims.

22. Discuss the use of slogans, maxims, and commandments in *Animal Farm*.

23. Discuss the concept of happiness, as it is presented in *Animal Farm*.

24. One critic has said that Orwell was happy while he was writing *Animal Farm*, partly because he was writing about animals, which he loved. Are there signs of this in the book?

25. Discuss the names Orwell chose for his characters.

26. Mr. Jones equals Czar Nicholas II. Do some research on this czar and discuss how closely you think Orwell used him as a model.

27. Describe the scene of Major's speech in purely human terms: what human types does Orwell describe during the speech? Do they represent a fair sampling of any given society? Why does the book begin with this audience?

28. What are the signs of inequality and oppression in the last two chapters? In the first chapter? What conclusion can you draw?

29. Make a list of lies that the pigs tell in the course of the book. Try to be representative rather than complete: what *kinds* of lies are told? Why?

Further Reading

CRITICAL WORKS

Crick, Bernard. *George Orwell: A Life*. London: Penguin, 1982.

Dyson, A.E. *The Crazy Fabric: Essays in Irony*. New York: St. Martin's, 1965.

Kernan, Alvin, editor. *Modern Satire*. New York: Harcourt Brace, 1962.

Lee, Robert A. *Orwell's Fiction*. Notre Dame: University of Notre Dame Press, 1972.

Williams, Raymond, editor. *George Orwell: A Collection of Critical Essays*. Englewood Cliffs: Prentice-Hall, 1974. Read especially Stephen J. Greenblatt's "Orwell as Satirist."

––––––. *George Orwell*. New York: Columbia University Press, 1981.

Woodcock, George. *The Crystal Spirit*. Boston: Little Brown, 1966.

AUTHOR'S OTHER WORKS

Orwell's books that will shed the most light on *Animal Farm* are *Homage to Catalonia* (1938) and *1984* (1949). Orwell's other principal works include:

Novels

Burmese Days   (1934)
A Clergyman's Daughter   (1935)
Keep the Aspidistra Flying   (1936)
Coming Up for Air   (1939)

Essay Collections

Inside the Whale   (1940)
Critical Essays   (1946)
Shooting an Elephant   (1950)

Autobiography

Down and Out in Paris and London (1933)
Such, Such Were the Joys (1953)

Miscellaneous

The Road to Wigan Pier (1937)

The Critics

Use of Fable and Allegory

In *Animal Farm*, [Orwell] chose for the first time an unrealistic, expressionistic device, the beast fable, as his satiric vehicle. The beast fable—a very ancient satiric technique—is basically the dramatic realization of metaphor; in a realistic work a man might be called a pig, but in the beast fable he is presented as an actual pig. Satirists have always found this translation of metaphor to dramatic fact an extremely effective way of portraying the true nature of vice and folly.

—Alvin Kernan, in *Modern Satire*, 1962

By transferring the problems of caste division outside a human setting, Orwell was able in *Animal Farm* to avoid the psychological complications inevitable in a novel, and thus to present his theme as a clear and simple political truth.

—George Woodcock, *The Crystal Spirit*, 1966

The allegory is very precise in its use of the major figures and incidents of the Russian Revolution. It expresses quite nakedly and with a complete lack of intellectual argument those aspects of Stalinism that most disturbed Orwell. At the same time the humbleness and warmth of the narrative give an attractive obliqueness without turning the direction of the satire. We can feel compassion for Orwell's creatures in a way that we cannot for Winston Smith, for the stark narrative of *1984* stuns our capacity for reaction. But *Animal Farm* is equally relentless in its message.

—Jenni Calder, *Chronicles of Conscience*, 1968

A Broader Meaning?

. . . this grim little parable is by no means about Russia alone. Orwell is concerned to show how revolutionary ideals of justice, equality and fraternity always shatter in the event. The ironic reversals in *Animal Farm* could be fairly closely related to real events since the work was written—this is not the least of their effectiveness—as well as to the events on which they were based . . .

A.E. Dyson, *The Crazy Fabric: Essays in Irony,* 1965

It is not merely that revolutions are self-destructive—Orwell also is painting a grim picture of the human condition in the political twentieth century, a time which he has come to believe marks the end of the very concept of human freedom. . . . At the end, all the representatives of the various ideologies are indistinguishable—they are all pigs, all pigs are humans. Communism is no better and no worse than capitalism or fascism; the ideals of socialism were long ago lost in Clover's uncomprehending gaze over the farm . . . perhaps more distressing yet is the realization that everyone, the good and the bad, the deserving and the wicked, are not only contributors to the tyranny, are not only powerless before it, but are unable to understand it . . . The potential hope of the book is finally expressed only in terms of ignorance (Boxer), wistful inarticulateness (Clover), or the tired, cynical belief that things never change (Benjamin). The inhabitants of this world seem to deserve their fate.

Robert A. Lee, *Orwell's Fiction,* 1969

[*Animal Farm*] has taken its place alongside *Candide* and *Gulliver's Travels* as one of those parables which embody permanent truths: a myth that will long outlast the particular historical events which form its background. Now that it is possible to view the work in context, freed of the emotional circumstances surrounding its publication, we can recognize it for what it is: a dystopia [an anti-utopia, an imaginary picture of the worst possible world], a satirical commentary upon human societies which vividly recalls Swift's . . .

J.R. Hammond, *A George Orwell Companion,* 1982

Orwell on *Animal Farm*

What I have most wanted to do throughout the past ten years is to make political writing into an art. My starting point is always a feeling of partisanship, a sense of injustice. When I sit down to write a book, I do not say to myself, "I am going to produce a work of art." I write it because there is some lie that I want to expose, some fact to which I want to draw attention, and my initial concern is to get a hearing. But I could not do the work of writing a book, or even a long magazine article, if it were not also an esthetic experience . . . So long as I remain alive and well I shall continue to feel strongly about prose style, to love the surface of the earth, and to take pleasure in solid objects and scraps of useless information.

. . . The problem of language is subtler and would take too long to discuss. I will only say that of late years I have tried to write less picturesquely and more exactly. In any case I find that by the time you have perfected any style of writing, you have always outgrown it. *Animal Farm* was the first book in which I tried, with full consciousness of what I was doing, to fuse political purpose and artistic purpose into one whole.

—from "Why I Write"

NOTES